The Fitchburg Watch

The
Fitchburg Watch

History of a Masterpiece

Richard Meibers

To, David Penny

[signature: Richard Meibers]

Martin and Lawrence Press
Groton, Massachusetts
2002

Published by Martin and Lawrence Press
PO Box 682
Groton, MA 01450

ISBN 0-9721687-0-2
Meibers, Richard
The Fitchburg Watch
History of a Masterpiece/by Richard Meibers 1st ed.
Summary: Historical perspective of the American watch-
making industry, using a single mass-produced watch as a
focus. 1. American History 2. Antiques 3. Pocket
Watches 4. Industrial Revolution   I. Title

Printed in Canada

Dedicated to my sons, Pan and Damon

ACKNOWLEDGMENTS

I would like to thank a number of people for their invaluable help. First and foremost is Stephan B. Helfant, without whom this book would not have been written. Then, Frank Morrison of Fitchburg State College, and Mike Harrold, who both supplied me with historical data, each from his own vast store of knowledge. Betsy Hannula of the Fitchburg Historical Society provided me with a most gracious welcome to her treasure trove of data and artifacts. Floyd Kemske shared good advice on writing a history. Mitch Fava, Dave Coccoli, Charlie Wallace, Al Ferraris, Bradley Ross, Dan Haff, and the members of the NAWCC chapter known as the MIT group, all helped make it possible. George Collord practically overwhelmed me with information. Ramsey and Perdida of Martin and Lawrence Press gave very helpful advice on getting set up for publication. Jeremy Townsend of J.N. Townsend Publishing added more publishing wisdom. Sally Reed listened to me drone on for hours about this subject. Rose Meibers and Pheobe Hackett did a great job of proofreading. And the Main Street Cafe in Groton provided endless hours of table space, complete with excellent coffee and bagels that stimulated conversation much in the same way the London coffee houses did for Boswell and Johnson.

Table of Contents

List of Photographs

PREFACE

A few years ago, I was invited on a tour of the Chelsea Clock Company in the small city of Chelsea that borders Boston. After the tour, the group I was with all decided to get a bite to eat in a nearby diner. During a conversation with the fellow sitting next to me, he said, seemingly out of the blue, "Never have so few done so much for so many" and asked me if I recognized those words. After I identified the quote as something Winston Churchill said about the RAF in the Battle of Britain, he showed me the wristwatch he was wearing.

The watch was not necessarily what might be considered a piece of jewelry, but it had a sturdy, utilitarian look to it. My lunch mate informed me that it was standard issue to all RAF pilots in World War II, and then proceeded to give a synopsis of the history of that infamous battle. Eating my plate of fried clam strips, I could not take my eyes off his watch as he related to me this fascinating story. His watch, every bit as accurate in 1999 as it was in 1942, provided me with a touchstone that brought the history an immediacy it might not otherwise have had.

That immediacy is the point of this book. It is the story of a single pocket watch, of how that pocket watch came to be. The watch itself is the focal point of a larger picture, a picture of what some believe to be one of the most important eras in the development of the United States as a world super power.

This story of the Fitchburg Watch can be appreciated by those horological aficionados who can satisfy their historical curiosity with an encapsulated overview of the atmosphere that gave rise to the American system of watch production. And it should also be enlightening to those with a more general interest in America's national history as well as that of local New England. That most important era of this country's development, the Industrial Revolution, can be seen through the window of this story, which turns, as Shakespeare says, the accomplishment of many years into an hour-glass. The manufacture of the Fitchburg Watch reflects the apogee of a revolution in technology, economics, and demographics that began in the early 1800s and laid the groundwork for the industrial age and led America to becoming a world power in the following century.

For anyone interested in nineteenth century American time pieces, this book will shed light on that group of watchmakers whose companies appeared on the scene for a short period of time, leaving only a small, but very significant, legacy behind. It speaks to the curiosity about some of the companies that have been listed in accounts of the watchmaking industry, but that, like the proverbial horse who starves to death waiting for the grass to grow, did not survive. This book will also place the mechanical watch and companies that manufactured these watches within the context of more general industrial development of the era.

The Fitchburg Watch is the figure against the background of the American Industrial Revolution. The picture of the revolution shown here is like an aerial view of a landscape, showing a broad vista of the scene. Like an aerial view, the picture is designed to show the reader the lay of the land without bringing into focus the thousands of intricate and complex details that have been covered in so many previously written volumes on the industrial age.

One outstanding detail of this broad industrial picture is a further snapshot of the development of the watch manufacturing industry in America, a development which helped lead the way and reflected the progress of the revolution.

Another, more detailed inset of the industrial picture is that of one of the age's early, important centers, Fitchburg, Massachusetts. This snapshot shows the transition from frontier outpost to farm community, and then, reflecting the very first beginnings of many such manufacturing sites, the city's maturation as a powerful industrial center by the latter end of the nineteenth century. As a further detailed inset, the city's development is reflected in the biographies of the two men who, in partnership with the city, founded the company that produced the Fitchburg Watch. Another close-up is the story of the company and the efforts to get it going, with details not previously recorded in any horological history. And finally, for those whose interest lie in the details of the mechanical timepiece, there is a close examination of the movement itself.

Just as there has been much written on the evolution of machine tools in the industrial age, there also exist many good books and articles on the technological development of the mechanical watch. For both the layman, as well as the technologically astute maven, this story will illuminate the climate and the mindset, as well as the trials and the pitfalls inherent in setting up an industrial enterprise in general, and a watch manufacturing company in particular. Technical terms and descriptions have been kept from being too detailed or esoteric, although certain mechanical descriptions germane to watchmaking are used.

The story of the Fitchburg Watch is factual. There are, however, places where educated guesses, suppositions and probabilities about people's behavior and motivations have been employed, using a judgment based on what action might be the most plausible in a given situation.

Chapter I

SELCHOW'S DISCOVERY

On August 15, 1968, a unique pocket watch turned up in an estate sale in Bedford, New Hampshire, among the personal effects of a recently deceased widow named Clara Lowe. The watch was bought by a man named Ted Koehler of Fitzwilliam, New Hampshire and later sold to a dealer in antique clocks, Gordon Boucher of Hillsboro, New Hampshire. Boucher, blessed with astute judgment and many years of experience dealing with the value of old family heirlooms, could tell that this watch was of good quality, and was a model of superb workmanship.

As usual, when buying a particular timepiece, Boucher had in mind certain collectors whom he knew might express interest in the item. Returning to his shop, one of the first people he phoned was a man named Fredrick Mudge Selchow, of Milford, New Hampshire. Over the years, Selchow had built a fairly large network of dealers and *pickers,* who would call him if something interesting showed up, and Boucher had, in the past, led him toward some very nice additions to his collection. Selchow responded by saying that it just so happened he would be driving by his neighborhood the next morning and would drop into his shop to see him.

Fred Selchow always responded in such a manner to that type of phone call. He didn't want to sound too avid, while at the same time making sure he got to the item of interest before anyone else did. During the forty-five-minute drive north from Milford to Hillsboro, he found his mind coming to rest on the name of the woman whose estate had been selling the collection of timepieces, trying to put his finger on what it was about the name Lowe that nagged at him. There was something he was forgetting. The name had a connection somewhere, with something he had read years before, but the connection now danced elusively just outside his consciousness. The morning was bright, the first cool day, normal for New England late summer mornings. For Selchow, even if the collection in Hillsboro held nothing which would be of interest to him, it was still a wonderful day for a drive.

Hillsboro sits among six different resort lakes and so its population swells in the summer months to twice what it is in the winter. In the fall, tour buses bring daily visitors to see the leaves turn color. Among the stores in the center of town, several antique shops do a thriving business with the summer vacationers, and with the leaf-peepers in the fall. At that time, Boucher's Antique Clocks occupied a cozy little spot in a row of stores on the corner of Main and Bridge Streets in the exact center of town. Fred Selchow arrived just as Boucher was opening his front door and shutting off the burglar alarm. They two men hadn't seen each other in close to a year, and they indulged themselves in some preliminary gossip about a rare clock that might be coming on the market. Then, against the background of no less that six clocks chiming the hour, Boucher displayed the recently acquired watch on a jeweler's bench in the rear of the long, narrow store.

The watch, larger than a 16 size but smaller than an 18, lay like a jewel in his hand. The solid gold hunter case opened to a ceramic dial with sunk seconds. The Roman numerals were long, in the American style, and the hour, minute and second hands were all blue scale spade. The dial face showed no company name, logo or other factory marking. Inside the back cover showed nice engine turning on the cuvette, and beautifully engraved rosettes around the two holes for key wind and key set. Under the cuvette, the engraving on the solid nickel top plate took him by surprise. In a beautiful hand, of a kind one doesn't see anymore, were the words "Union Watch Co." and "Fitchburg, Mass." The design and construction of the watch movement itself appeared to be quite beautiful, the damaskeening, as well as the engraving on the simple regulator, pleasing to the eye. He had seen watches engraved with the words "Union Watch Company" before along with the name of some city like New York or Boston. These had all been Swiss imitations of American-made watches, and none of them had ever contained the word "Fitchburg." Two other details caught his eye. First, the top plate had no serial number or date on it, and second, the screw pattern on the top plate was unusual. There were too many screws for a ¾ plate.

Clearly, from the workmanship that had gone into this watch, it was obviously not a cheap Swiss imitation and, though he wasn't exactly sure why, some instinct told him that what he held in his hand was a rare and exciting find. Like an experienced bargainer, he kept his excitement hidden as he laid the watch on the counter and, modulating his voice, he asked, "How much would you want for this?" After some haggling back and forth, they arrived at a price that each thought was fair. Or, more to the point, a price that each felt left himself at an advantage, much more than Boucher paid for the watch, but much less than Selchow suspected it was worth.

When the exchange was complete, Selchow looked closely at the movement of the watch again. "Look at that," he said, showing the engraved top plate to Boucher. "You ever seen anything like that before?"

Boucher leaned on his elbows at the edge of his jeweler's bench and looked closer at the watch. He shook his head. "I didn't know they made watches in Fitchburg."

"Supposedly, there was a company there for a few years in the late eighteen hundreds, but nobody's ever seen a watch from it."

"You think...?" Boucher raised his eyebrows, looking up at Selchow who shrugged and closed the cover, then placed the watch into a chamois pouch he carried with him for that purpose.

Driving back to Milford that brilliantly sunny afternoon was an exceptionally charged experience for Fred Selchow. There are many satisfactions in acquiring and owning a collection of any kind of antique, but there is probably nothing that equals the first tingle of discovery, knowing one has in his hands a little piece of history. Was it too much to hope that the watch he had just bought had actually been made by a company that collectors knew only as a mention in old books? But even if it wasn't what he hoped, at the very least he had had a good day; and bought a lovely specimen at a reasonable price. It would be a fine addition to his collection.

As soon as supper ended that evening, he retired to his library to find references to the watch company of Fitchburg. His library, which was also his museum, held one of the finest collections of antique clocks and watches in the entire country. Whether he was trying to acquire a particular timepiece for his collection or unearthing the history of a piece, Fred Selchow was known to dog his quarry like a hound on a scent. Small of stature with erect, somewhat military, posture and trim mustache, he traced his lineage back to Thomas Mudge, the eighteenth-century English watchmaker accredited with the invention of the lever escapement. Fortunately, Fred had the money and the leisure time to indulge his one great fascination, the collection of antique watches and clocks. His father had made the family fortune by developing and marketing the board game called *Parcheesi,* and he later owned the rights to another international favorite, *Trivial Pursuit.*

The words "Fitchburg, Mass" engraved on the top plate of the watch led him first to Charles Crossman's *A Complete History of Watchmaking in The United States,* published in 1888 as a compilation of articles written for a trade magazine of that time. Crossman wrote, "The Fitchburg Watch Company never really existed although all necessary preparation had been made in expectation of forming a watch company...Mr. Sylvanus Sawyer, one of the stockholders of the defunct United States Watch Company in Marion, New Jersey...conceived the idea...first by commencing the manufacture of tools and machinery...and when ready to commence the manufacture of watches to form a stock company."

For years collectors had kept their eyes open for a watch from this company, with a dwindling expectation of ever finding one. Also, in 1888, Henry Abbott wrote in *The Watch Factories of America*, "In the year 1875 Mr. S. Sawyer of Fitchburg, Mass. concluded to start a watch factory in the town in which he resided...He entered into negotiations with Mr. Henry J. Lowe...previously...a superintendent in the United States Watch Factory..." Henry J. Lowe! Was it possible that Clara Lowe and Henry J. Lowe were somehow related? That certainly seemed to Selchow to be a good place to start his attempts to trace this watch to the short-lived nineteenth-century company in Fitchburg. As any collector knows, the first thrill of discovery is always followed by the more sober realization that his recent serendipity just might not be what he hopes it to be, and that he has now to authenticate his find. If he could make the connection between Clara Lowe and Henry J. Lowe, he just might be able to trace this newly acquired watch to the Fitchburg company.

The following day the search began. The auctioneer who sold the estate goods turned out to be T.R. Langdell of Wilton, New Hampshire. Langdell billed himself as "New England's Biggest Auctioneer" (the man weighed close to four hundred and fifty pounds). Langdell put Selchow in touch with the lawyer for the estate, who in turn gave him the name of the executrix of the estate, a Mrs. Povey.

Mrs. Povey, it turned out, was Mrs. Lowe's sister and lived in Manchester, New Hampshire. "Yes, wasn't it tragic?" Mrs. Povey said on the phone. "Poor Clara being killed like that by a drunk driver who crossed the center line and hit her car head on. And her poor husband dying only last year." Mrs. Povey did remember the gold pocket watch belonging to Clara's husband, Carroll. It had been his grandfather's watch. No, she didn't know the grandfather's name. Carroll Lowe was such a nice man and good to her sister Clara. He died of pneumonia in Eliot Hospital in Manchester. They had no children; it was just the two of them. No, she didn't know where Carroll was born. He wasn't from New Hampshire, though.

The next stop, then, was Manchester, New Hampshire with its string of abandoned textile mills lining each bank of the Merrimack River. The clerk's office in city hall gave him a copy of Carroll Lowe's death certificate, listing his place of birth as Waltham, Massachusetts. Now he was getting someplace. Selchow headed down Route 93 to Massachusetts.

Waltham is one of many small cities in the Greater Boston area. Originally settled in the early 1600s on the banks of the Charles River, the city's history is linked inexorably to the Industrial Age in America. Beginning before the Industrial Revolution with its grist mills using river power, it has extended its influence well into the present-day Computer Revolution. Route 128, known as America's Technology Highway, runs through Waltham. What in the 1900s was home to innovations in machine technology is today home to innovations in computer, space, and missile technology. And, of course, it was home to the one company that made the city world-famous, the American Waltham Watch Company. In 1968, the old watch factory on the bank of the Charles River, as well as Francis Cabot Lowell's original textile mill, had the same abandoned look as the old textile mill buildings in Manchester. But there was talk of renovating the huge old brick buildings and making them into office and apartment complexes, with one section set aside for a museum of industry that might house a watch museum. The watch museum exists today on a balcony above the Museum of Industry, in what had once been the original textile factory across the river and downstream of the old Waltham Watch Company building.

At the Waltham city hall Fred Selchow obtained a copy of Carroll Lowe's birth certificate, which showed that he had been born in 1893, his mother, Rose Wright, born in Lunenburg, his father Frank Preston Lowe, job master at the American Waltham Watch Company, born in Fitchburg, Massachusetts. Frank Lowe's death certificate, found in the same office, showed that he had, like his son, died of pneumonia. If Fred Selchow was a demonstrative man he might have made a little hop of joy at the next piece of information found on the death certificate. Frank Lowe's father was indeed Henry J. Lowe of Fitchburg.

So, the connection of the watch to the Fitchburg Watch Company was made. Passed down to his grandson, the watch had been owned by the man whom both Crossman and Abbott had listed as the superintendent of the company. Satisfied with a good day's work, Fred Selchow headed for home.

The genealogical path from Clara Lowe to Henry J. Lowe may have led Selchow in the right direction but it was not necessarily smoking-gun proof that this watch was manufactured in the Fitchburg factory. He needed to look further to establish that proof. Perhaps there was some detail of the watch itself that could tell him something about where and when it was made. At home that evening he put the watch on his jeweler's bench for a closer examination.

Several clues indicated this to be a high quality watch. The case was solid gold and obviously custom-made. The jewel settings were beveled and highly polished. The watch company of Fitchburg was supposed to have existed from the year 1875 to the year 1878. The 16 and 17 size American watches were relatively rare in the 1870s. Up to the 1880s, eighty-five percent of the watches made in this country were the 18 size. First made around 1860, the 16 size, which for marketing purposes included the 17 size, gained very slowly in popularity up into the twentieth century as the earlier more fashionable 18 size diminished. If this watch were manufactured in the 1870s it was a little ahead of its time. Since no serial number showed on the top plate, or anywhere else on the watch, it was not made as one of a series. As a stand-alone, the movement must have been a prototype, used either for display or as a model on which subsequent pieces could be patterned. Of course, the movement could have come from anywhere, with the words "Fitchburg, Mass" and "Union Watch Company" later engraved on the top plate by Henry Lowe. He lived in Fitchburg, and the Union Watch Company could have been some dream of his, to start another company at a different time. But, in that case, Lowe would have put a serial number or a date on the watch. And as far as Selchow knew, a Union Watch Company had never existed in Fitchburg.

The screw pattern on the top plate, which Selchow had noticed the first time he looked at the watch, consisted of five screws for just one plate, besides the two case screws. This seemed very unusual, as well as unnecessary for a 3/4 plate. He had never seen another example of such a thing. The 3/4 plate itself suggested that the watch was more likely to have been made in the 1880s or 1890s when the fashion for the 3/4 plate reached its peak, again suggesting it may have been ahead of its time if it was made in the 1870s. That the watch was key-wound and key-set suggested that it might have been made earlier than the 1880s since the trend in American watches—unlike their European counterparts—toward stem wind rose precipitously in that decade so that by 1890 almost ninety percent of watches made in America were stem wound. The fashion for 15 jewels in some of the better watches climbed throughout the 1870s and 1880s to reach its peak in 1890, so there was a decent probability that a good watch produced in the middle 1870s would have 15 jewels like the one Selchow had in his hands. And there was no question that this was one of the better watches, one that any watchmaker would be proud to carry for his own use.

For comparison, Selchow pulled from his collection other 16 or 17 size watches from that period. One watch stood out because of its similarity to the Lowe watch. This example, engraved with the name Edwin Rollo, came from a series manufactured by the United States Watch Company in Marion, New Jersey. The serial number told him that it was made in 1873. The United States Watch Company listed the Edwin Rollo as a 16 size. On measuring the movement, however, Selchow determined that it was actually 17 size, exactly the same size as the Lowe watch. It had a 1/4 plate and bridge movement, and much to his surprise, the top plate used the exact same pattern of five screws as did the Lowe watch. On the United States Watch Company's example, however, the screw pattern made sense. Three screws were used to hold the plate that covered the going train and the other two were for a separate barrel bridge.

Selchow went through his collection and then did a thorough search of his literature to see if he could find another top plate by any other manufacturer with the same screw pattern. The only watches he could find with the same pattern, a John W. Lewis and another engraved with just the name United States Watch Company, were both made by the company in Marion, New Jersey, but with higher serial numbers than the Edwin Rollo. They were both listed as 16 size, 15 jewel, 1/4 plate and bridge, and must have been made in late 1873 or early 1874, just before the Marion company filed for bankruptcy.

The next step was to dismantle the Lowe watch and the Edwin Rollo to see if the parts were interchangeable. They were. All the steel work, the pillar plate, minute and hour wheels, cannon pinion, winding wheel and click were absolutely identical, besides the screw pattern being entirely interchangeable. Furthermore, he could see that the milling of the dial side of the pillar plate was done by the same machinery.

Was it possible that the Lowe watch was actually made at the United States Watch Company's factory and then engraved and put in a case in Fitchburg by Henry Lowe? Yes, it was possible, but there was another, more probable, answer. Both Crossman and Abbott state, in their histories of the United States Watch Company, that at the time of the company's bankruptcy in 1875, a good portion of their watch machinery was sold to three different companies, the Fredonia Watch Company of New York, the Auburndale Watch Company of Massachusetts, and the Fitchburg Watch Company. Putting all this together, Fred Selchow came to the most probable conclusion that the watch from the Clara Lowe estate was indeed manufactured by the Fitchburg Watch Company. Henry

J. Lowe, who had been the superintendent of the United States Watch Company, left there when the company went bankrupt. From there he went to Fitchburg where he took the position of superintendent of the newly-formed watch company. He brought with him machinery to make a 17 size watch. The watch that Selchow held in his hand was made with that machinery.

Now Fred Selchow could let himself feel the full effect of the first tingle of excitement he had experienced on seeing the watch for the first time in Boucher's shop. He was indeed holding in his hand an important piece of American history. He put what he now could call the Fitchburg watch back together. His wife had gone to bed hours earlier, sticking her head in the door of his study to tell him not to stay up too late. He put his books and his watchmaker's tools away and then sat for a while just looking at the newest addition to his collection. It was indeed a beautiful watch. It was well worth the money he had paid for it even without a history attached. He opened the back and set the time with a key, and he wound the watch, also with the key. Three minutes till midnight. It was late and he was tired. But what a full and satisfying day he had.

Over the next few weeks he called several of his friends who were also collectors of watches and clocks. He called for two reasons. One was to give them the facts that led him to the conclusion he had formed, and to ask them if they could think of any reason why he should not form this conclusion. And, second, he wanted to brag just a little bit. Each in turn, his friends said that, yes, they completely agreed with his conclusions and each congratulated him on his find. The following spring he published his finding in the Bulletin of the National Association of Watch and Clock Collectors.

In the Smithsonian Institute in Washington there is today a display of American watch manufacturers. Each company has its own spot in the display along with its representative watches. There has been a spot and a superficial description of the Fitchburg watch company, but there has never been a representative watch on display there. After finding the first watch, Fred Selchow always maintained that there must be others. The company existed for approximately four years. Some machinery was already owned and other machinery obviously built. Skilled watchmakers, besides Henry Lowe, came from the United States Watch Company to work there. Capital money was put up by Sylvanus Sawyer to get the operation off the ground. But no other watch from that company has ever been found.

*Top plate of the Fitchburg Watch
showing the five screw pattern*

*Top plate on the Edwin Rollo
showing the same screw pattern*

The Fitchburg Machine Company, in a factory built by Sylvanus Sawyer in 1866. The building exists today on lower Main Street as a warehouse and outlet for the Fitchburg Plumbing Supply.

Chapter 2

THE SECOND AMERICAN REVOLUTION

The Fitchburg watch remained in Fred Selchow's collection until he passed away in 1988. A private collector in the Fitchburg area acquired the watch from his estate and has owned it ever since. After the watch surfaced in the sixties many collectors searched in vain for other Fitchburg watches. The collector who now has the watch had scoured the surrounding towns for years for a specimen from the Fitchburg company before acquiring Selchow's watch, and he took up the search again after 1988. The flurry died down eventually, but, despite great effort, not another product from the watch company of Fitchburg has ever been found. But, because of Selchow's discovery, the dream of finding another authentic Fitchburg watch has loomed much like the old prospectors' dreams of finding a lost gold mine. A small cadre of veteran watch collectors will still, to this day, when attending an estate auction or browsing through an antique shop anywhere in Massachusetts, New Hampshire or western Connecticut, or searching the web, keep an eye out for the words "Fitchburg, Mass" engraved on a top plate. As late as the spring of the year 2001, an ad appeared in the *Fitchburg Sentinel* requesting any information about a pocket watch bearing such an inscription.

Unlike any other book you are likely to read on the subject of pocket watch manufacture, this book is not about a company's product line, or even a particular model of watch. This is about one single watch. But on the other hand, it is not about a one-of-a-kind that an individual watchmaker, in his shop on Main Street, might have assembled with parts obtained from various providers and then inserted into a case from yet another maker. This story focuses on one watch, made on machinery designed to mass-produce five, or twenty, or two hundred watches a day, but for whatever reason, produced only one. Such is the watch that Fred Selchow acquired in Hillsboro, New Hampshire in 1968.

You might be wondering: why a book about just one watch? If you are a watch collector, your interest is more likely to tend toward advances in watch technology and design, or in completing a particular set of Walthams, Howards, or Elgins, or maybe a certain kind of regulator or escapement. What could be interesting about a watch that, as far as anyone knows, was the only product of a company that expired in gestation? After all, the Fitchburg watch, albeit a very beautiful piece of craftsmanship, is not the Koh-i-noor diamond. So what's the big deal?

The importance of this watch is that it exists as a symbol, or a focal point of an era. By looking at the background story behind the production of this one watch we can see America's Industrial Revolution, that revolution's geography, attitudes, technology, economics, and the kind of society that made it possible. And there is no argument that America's industrial development is what led the way to the country's rise to its position as the supreme power in the world today.

The jewel that sat at the pinnacle of machine technology in nineteenth-century America was the mass produced pocket watch. It is analogous to the diamond. Ninety-nine percent of all the diamonds that are mined in the world are used for industrial purposes, for grinders, drill heads, polishers, etc. These diamonds, the hardest substance found on the planet, are carbon black and are mined exclusively for industrial uses. That other one percent, the translucent ones, some with flaws, some not, are those that are prized and worn as jewelry. In pretty much the same way, we think of machinery as being used in some kind of work, whether it's industrial manufacturing or farming or construction or transportation or in a domestic household. But that tiny percent of all machinery, the clock and, to an even finer degree, the pocket watch, do nothing more than measure the ephemeral quantity of time and, also, like the translucent diamond, are used as adornment and jewelry.

The definition of a machine, as opposed to a hand tool, is that, once set in motion and given a constant power supply, the machine will continue functioning until it is either shut off, or the power runs out, or the machine's parts are worn out from use. An early grist mill, driven by a waterwheel, was a machine. An early treadle-powered lathe was not. The workings of a watch, from the power supply of either a wound spring or a quartz, through the escapement to the various wheels, and then to the hour, minute and second hands is a machine, which, by the latter part of the industrial revolution, had become a very precise machine. For people of the nineteenth century, as awed and enamored of the machine as we are today of the computer, to be able to carry this tiny, beautiful and precise machine in their pocket certainly gave them a sense of satisfaction and prestige beyond its utility in getting them to the train station on time.

Since the Fitchburg Watch is the only single watch to come out of mass production, oxymoron that it is, it will allow us to focus in on how it came to be, without the great distraction of how the company subsequently grew and competed in what was a highly competitive market. The city of Fitchburg, Massachusetts, where the watch was made, affords a microcosm of the industrial age. Starting out like thousands of other farm towns in the eighteenth century, the city's growth exactly coincides with America's industrial growth till it peaks in the late nineteenth century, levels off and then begins its decline in the twentieth century. Unlike other major industrial centers in this country, it never became anything else. That's not to say that the city never will become anything else. Even as I write this there are plans afoot for new electronics industries along the Nashua River. But the fertile soil of Fitchburg's industry has lain fallow for a long enough time as to isolate it from its former bumper crop of machine shops, textile and paper mills, and tool and weapons factories. It is against the background of America's Industrial Revolution that the city of Fitchburg and its life as an industrial center needs to be looked at. The kind of city that Fitchburg became could have flourished only in an era of growing manufacture. The

20

watch company of Fitchburg can be seen like a *bas relief*, standing out from an historical map of the city. A company like this could only have happened in a city like Fitchburg.

THE AMERICAN SYSTEM OF MANUFACTURE

The term "Industrial Revolution" was originally popularized by the historian Arnold Toynbee to describe Britain's economic development from 1760 to 1840, by which time the country had matured into the world's first fully industrialized nation. The term is used to describe the impact that technological change has made throughout the entire world, an impact that, like no other phenomenon in the recorded history of mankind has changed the lives of every person living in a civilized society. One point on which every economist would agree is Karl Marx's statement that the Industrial Revolution catapulted the Western world into a new age of prosperity never before witnessed in history. The economist, John Maynard Keynes, wrote in 1930 that "From the earliest times of which we have record…down to the beginning of the eighteenth century there was no very great change in the standard of living of the average man…" But as a result of the next two centuries, "the average standard of life in Europe and the United States has been raised fourfold" and would raise again four to eight times what it was in the 1930s.

Prior to the eighteenth century, technological improvements had, for most of the world, lain dormant since the Renaissance. By the early nineteenth century the revolution had extended from England to Belgium and

France and then Germany. The newly formed United States experienced the first stirrings of the revolution in the 1790s, and by the time it reached its manufacturing maturity in the latter part of the nineteenth century, had already outdistanced all of Europe in industrial might.

Before the American colonies were able to gain their independence from England, their involvement in the new industrial age was mostly limited to providing a market for British goods and, to a lesser extent, providing raw materials for the mother country's factories. Realizing the technical and economic power their new factory system gave them, the British had passed strict laws forbidding the exportation of machinery, skilled workers, and manufacturing know-how to other countries, as well as to their own colonies.

The change in America from the agricultural society of the eighteenth century to an industrial society took the better part of the nineteenth century to complete. The beginnings of this change can be seen in writings of such statesmen as Thomas Jefferson and Alexander Hamilton. Jefferson wrote that "agriculture has intrinsically a strong claim to pre-eminence over every other kind of industry." It was partially on the basis of this sentiment that his administration was voted into office in 1800. Hamilton took the opposing view, that the real interests of the country "will be advanced…by the due encouragement of manufactures." The rise of manufacturing occurred at a rapid pace during Jefferson's term in office and beyond. By 1816, as an elder statesman, but still the owner of extensive farmlands and at least 600 slaves, his writings reveal an enthusiastic acceptance of the country's new industries.

From 1820 to 1840, the population on America's farms grew by 97%. In the cities and the new manufacturing centers, it grew by 127%. Political power in Washington, though, still resided with the agricultural sector of the country since the new western states which were added—there were 24 states by 1830—were all agriculturally based. The great rise in manufacturing occurred in only one section of the country—New England. With its barren soil, inexhaustible water supply, dense population, and Yankee mechanical ingenuity, the area staged Act II of the Shot Heard 'Round the World.

When the Industrial Revolution came to the United States in the early nineteenth century, it mirrored the changes in British society. With the extensive use of water power, the subsequent utilization of steam power, and revisions to machinery used to manufacture goods from raw materials like cotton or iron, the revolution changed America's face forever. It created a new way of working, a new economics, and a new class of worker. In the seventeenth and early eighteenth century, like Britain prior to the middle 1700s, manufactured items were hand-produced by single craftsmen or in small shops where a master craftsman might oversee and train one or more apprentices. In some instances, like the watch and clock industry where the manufactured item was a little more complex, separate parts such as wheels, pinions or arbors might be made in different cottages and then sent to the timepiece maker's shop for assembly and adjustment. Industrialization brought all these workers together into *manufacturies*, creating a new way of life and what came to be known as the American System of Manufacture. Beginning with Francis Cabot Lowell's first textile mill in Waltham, in the very early years of the century, many brought their operation under one roof.

The American System owes much of its eventual overwhelming success to the very new, special relationship between the skills of the mechanic and those of the entrepreneur. While charting new realms of endeavor, if these two very separate skills were not embodied in the same person, then they were in two people who worked closely together and knew each other well. Success on any level led to reinvestment of profits, which brought about improved technology. By 1868, even the British were beginning to emulate this new approach. An article in the London Times, describing the "first English watch manufactory" states that they "followed the example of the Americans...whereby a saving in cost of one-third is effected." Watchmaking by machine, as with the manufacture of such items as clothing and furniture, is mass production of a product not designed to fit an individual customer and therefore is not tied directly to orders or sales. The financial risk involved in this type of manufacture is substantial compared to the making of, for example, a locomotive or a battleship, where the order is taken and money is received from the customer before the work begins.

THE SEEDS OF CHANGE

In the early years of the newly-formed United States, the transition from farm to factory was spurred by several factors. The American farmer himself was a wonderfully diverse and creative tinkerer who developed an open-minded attitude toward the work in his farm's machine shop, an attitude kept from workers in England by the restrictions of that country's craftsman guilds. The freedom of this open-minded creativity in America led to a flood of inventions and patents, first filed in the United States in 1790. Because of the wide range of skills needed on frontier farms, a farmer might encompass many different professions when given the freedom to do so. From repairing the metal connections on his horse's harness, he might move to silversmithing and from that to watch repair. John Fitch, a cousin to the man for whom Fitchburg is named, and an early inventor of the steamboat in 1785, went from his father's farm in Connecticut to making clocks, then became a brass founder, later a silversmith, and a gunsmith. After seeing his steamboat invention copied by Robert Fulton, he gave up that pursuit in disgust, and moved west to the Ohio and Kentucky territories where he became a cartographer, and later an engraver. Another classic example of this kind of diversity was Paul Revere who went from being a silversmith before making his famous ride, to manufacturing boilers for Fulton's steamboats in the later part of his life. Farmers were also artisans, making their own guns, pottery, furniture, fabrics, clothing, and processed foods. They were quite often lumberers and operators of both sawmills and grist mills. Many advances in mill technology and the use of water power were achieved by these early Yankee farmers.

On a few occasions, technological knowledge was successfully spirited past England's laws and brought across the ocean, most notably by Samuel Slater whose experience with spinning and carding machines made possible the opening of the first textile mill in Pawtucket, Rhode Island in 1789. The technology of the steam engine had first found its way to America in 1753, to be used in a New Jersey mine shaft. Even though prodigious use of steam engines was inhibited by the widespread utilization of water, especially in New England, steam engine technology, when it finally caught hold, made great strides in the United States due to the vast supply of firewood not available to the British. By 1793 there were three functioning steam engines in the United States. These noisy, sputtering monsters, which seemed to have a life of their own, were so fearsome to people unused to machinery that at the end of the eighteenth century, as Philadelphia planned to install a steam-powered water works to provide drinking water for the city, its engineer had to assure the public that "a steam engine is, at present, as tame and innocent as a clock." These kind of statements may have been good for the public's gradual acceptance of steam power, but stringent public safety codes needed to be passed because the early steam boiler was, in fact, a literal bomb that could be extremely dangerous.

Technological innovations were spurred by economic necessity. President Jefferson's imposition of steep tariffs on British imports, just after the turn of the century, prompted many retailers to look for alternative, less costly suppliers closer to home. The President's embargo of English goods hurt many prosperous mercantile businesses, like that of Francis Cabot Lowell in Boston. It was this downturn in his business that provided the impetus for the building of America's first large textile plant in Waltham, Massachusetts, which later moved to the banks of the Merrimac River where the mill village of his workers grew eventually to become the city that bears his name.

In some cases, the growth in manufacturing was promoted by peddlers sent out to help instill a need for a product. Eli Terry of Connecticut, who manufactured clocks with wooden movements, at first piled them on wagons and traveled about the countryside selling them to farmers and shopkeepers. A clock was more than just a timepiece, he realized, it helped define a person's social standing. Even if it didn't keep good time, it marked its owner as one of the landed gentry. Merchants and Yankee peddlers carried them as part of their usual line of goods. The merchants Levi and Edward Porter in Waterbury, Connecticut sold 4000 of Terry's wooden movement clocks in the few years after 1810. While they did not yet have interchangeable parts, Terry's clocks, followed by Eli Whitney's muskets in New Haven, Connecticut were the first mass-produced items in America. Terry set up a factory for machine-manufactured clocks, and sold the business to Seth Thomas in 1822. In 1836 alone, that company turned out and sold 80,000 wooden-movement clocks.

As industry grew, more and varied groups came to rely on the artificial marking of time. Economic rhythms overpowered the rhythms of nature. A farmer traditionally marked his time with the rising and setting of the sun and with seasons of the year, but a manufacturer needed another kind of time. If he was to have a labor force working together in his factory, he needed them all to be there at the same time. He also needed to know when his raw materials would arrive by train or by steamboat. Sail powered boats moved in and out of their ports on a time schedule based on the wind and tides, but when Robert Fulton's steamboats began plying the Hudson River in

1807, its cargo customers and its passengers needed to know when the boat would arrive.

In 1800, about one in every ten homes in America had a clock, and about one in every thirty-two people owned a watch. Most people told time by the clock in the town square, on the church steeple. With the coming of the new brass manufacturing industry in Connecticut, the clock movements could be made faster and less expensively than the wooden movements. As industries grew, the town clocks were mounted on a tower of the factory itself for the benefit of the workers in the mill village.

THE MACHINES

In the early decades of the nineteenth century, invention and innovation became the rule. From the 1850s through the 1870s, the increase in the number of manufacturing patents registered was far greater than at any other time in the history of the United States. Just as in the early 1980s when people were beginning to understand the seemingly limitless possibilities for the use of computers as a tool, in the middle 1800s they were learning all the new things they could do with the more efficient harnessing of water power, and then later the use of steam power. In a factory, the lathes, screw machines, and drilling machines could be hooked up to a central power conduit allowing the individual worker at each machine to increase production by a thousand times over what a man could do with his bow lathe. With the new self-acting machine, hooked to a power conduit with all the turning power he needed, and two free hands to make his piece, he could turn out in a minute what he used to turn out in an hour. In some cases where many different set-ups were not involved, he could do in a minute what it used to take an entire day.

Again, like the computer industry of this century, the American watch manufacturing industry, beginning in the middle of the nineteenth century, was driven by technological innovation. It was not dependent on bulk raw materials like, for example, the textile or wood product industries. Shipping and distribution were only minor considerations for watchmakers. So, a small watch factory like Luther Goddard's in Shewsbury, Massachusetts or the Pitkin brother's in Hartford, Connecticut could be set up just about anywhere. Begun in the early part of the nineteenth century, both these companies turned out a small number of good watches, the small number owing to their lack of adequate water or steam power and the machinery innovations that came later. By the 1850s, companies like the American Watch Company in Waltham and the E. Howard & Co. in Boston began making what would become the finest mass-produced watches in the world. Twenty years later, even a fledgling start-up company, with the proper tools, 2500 square feet of factory space, a one cylinder steam engine and a skilled labor force, could turn out up to twenty watches a day.

The largest expenditure of time and money in setting up a watch factory was the acquisition or the manufacture of adequate machine tools to make the various parts of the movements. Henry Pitkin, between 1834 and 1838, designed and built some of the first machine tools for watch manufacture. His machines were forerunners of later, more complex models built for the Waltham and

Howard companies in the 1850s. In later years, many of these more complex machines might pass from one company that had fallen on hard times to a new one just starting up. In a watchmaking factory the most important workers, next to the adjusters who regulated the watches, were the machinists who designed, built, and repaired the tools used in production. If steam power can be said to have been the driving energy behind the Industrial Age, the machine tools, the lathes and milling machines, were the vehicles that carried it. Again, this is roughly analogous to our own Electronic Age where the microchip and the circuit board provide the vehicle for carrying the innovations in software technology. In the watch industry of the nineteenth century, modifications in watch design were like our advances in software design. Just as upgrades in software would not be possible without changes and advances in hardware, a new design for a watch would not have been possible without at least one, if not several, modifications in the design of the machine tools used in making the watches.

It could be said that the Industrial Revolutions of Europe and the United States were the result of four factors, (a) iron production, (b) development of the steam engine, (c) mass production, and (d) the development of precision machine tools. In the production of iron, America once again had a large advantage over Europe because of the enormous quantities of wood available in North America. Reducing iron ore to pig iron using charcoal made from wood is vastly superior to the use of coal due to the impurities in the iron produced, which were caused by the coal.

In the middle of the nineteenth century, England had the greatest industrial economy in the world, and so was shocked to find, at the Crystal Palace exhibition in London in 1851, a demonstration of what became known as the "American System," the technique of interchangeable parts in the construction of firearms. By the time of the exhibition, this style of manufacturing had spread in America, and began to dominate fabrication of products from hardware to sewing machines, clocks and watches. The interchangeable part was not the only mark of advanced American technique. The United States led the way not only in the manufacture of machines and machine tools, but also in assembly line production. Conveyor belts were first used in flour processing plants and in slaughterhouses. The earliest one, in Cincinnati in the 1840s, moved hogs from one station to the next, permitting specialization in labor as well as saving time and human effort in moving the carcass from one work station to another. The movement of these carcasses along the conveyor belt gave rise to a popular local song entitled "Cincinnati's Dancing Pig."

The machine shop was central to the story of production in almost every industry. The development of precision machine tools began and continued in Europe, but once America achieved a full separation from its colonial past, it began to hold its own in this area and eventually surpassed everyone but the Germans in the latter part of the nineteenth century. Machine tools can be broken down into different categories; the lathe; the grinder; the milling machine; the wire drawer; and the gear-cutter, which is actually a type of milling machine.

The lathe, along with the bow drill, is one of the two oldest machine tools used by man. It was known to exist as far back as 2500 BC in Egypt, and was also employed by the Etruscans as long ago as 700 BC. However, lathes were used only as woodworking tools until late in the eighteenth century. Diagrams of screw-cutting lathes can be found in Leonardo da Vinci's drawings, and depictions of pole-and-treadle lathes are found throughout the Middle Ages. Early lathes were powered by bows, hand cranks, foot treadles, or cord-driven great wheels. They developed closer and better tolerances due to use in the clock, watch, and instrument making industry, and were transformed into industrial tools in the eighteenth century, mostly in France and Germany, for the explicit purpose of cutting tiny precision screws and fusees for watches. The watchmaker's bow-driven lathe was called a "turn" because the cutting needed for a small watch part required nothing more than a simple turn of the wheel.

From 1800 on, the lathe was developed into a tool for working with iron and steel. The industrial lathe was developed in England, most notably by Henry Maudsley. The first American development of the lathe is an early design as a screw-making machine for Slater's mill in Rhode Island in the 1790's. David Wilkinson, designer of Slater's lathe which was powered by a water mill, went on to produce hundreds of lathes sold to newly-formed factories throughout New England. In 1852, the burgeoning watch manufacturing industry saw the development of a revolutionary advancement in lathe technology. Charles Moseley, a machine tool designer for the new Boston Watch Company in Roxbury, Massachsetts, built a lathe with a split collet and a draw piece for holding the material to be worked on. Prior to that time, material to be worked on was attached to the head of the lathe—or mandrel as it was called—by shellac, making for a tenuous hold as the material was turned. The split collet and draw piece, which quickly became the standard for all industries and is still used to this day, held the material firmly in place thereby saving countless hours both in set-up time and in redoing ruined material. In the watchmaking industry, various precision lathes were developed in the middle 1800's for mass-producing interchangeable parts. Each individual watch part usually had its own lathe or a series of different lathes, some for arbors and staffs, others for jewels, and others for screw-making. The watch manufacturer's lathes were made heavy for their size to give stability and long wear, and many lathes went from one watch company to another, some in use well into the twentieth century.

A different genre of tool, the grinding machine, has been in use since the Neolithic Period (15,000-5000 BC). Until the end of the eighteenth century, though, the grinder was used primarily for sharpening and polishing, but by the middle of the nineteenth century, the grinding machine appeared as a precision manufacturing instrument. It is a very different kind of tool than a lathe or a drill which both use a single point to do their job. A grinding machine uses an abrasive type wheel containing many small points. The first industrial grinder that could be called a machine tool appeared in 1830 but was not refined until the 1840s when it was used in making Elias Howe's new sewing machines. The sewing machine was the first complex instrument to come into the American home since the clock and had the same basic need, that of precise and consistent repetitive movement. In the clock, the movement of the hands recorded accurate time and in the sewing machine the movement of the needle and the advancement of the cloth produced an accurate stitch. The sewing machine needed to be light, since it was used by women. It also needed to last a long time, and was actually the first home purchase to be financed on time payments.

High precision grinding was first seen in the watchmaking industry in Europe as early as the 1820s. In 1860 Charles Moseley designed a grinding machine for the Nashua Watch Company that was later brought to the American Waltham Watch Company where it was used until 1872, and then replaced by a more accurate grinding machine. Moseley's machine was stored in a warehouse, kept as a back-up for several years, until it was bought by the United States Watch Company of Waltham and used until 1889. Today this machine is in the possession of the Norton Company where it is displayed in their museum in Worcester, Massachusetts.

The Johnny-come-lately of the precision machine tools is the milling machine, the development of which was accomplished almost entirely in the United States, first in New England and then in the Midwest, most notably in Cincinnati. Similar machines were used by clockmakers in France in the seventeenth and eighteenth centuries and by makers of locks in England in the early nineteenth century. The first crude milling machines were made in this county in 1818 by Eli Whitney for his gun factory in Connecticut. Later, crude models were developed for specific purposes, and the first universal milling machine was produced by Brown & Sharpe of Providence, Rhode Island in 1861. However, the true precision milling machine did not appear until the 1870s.

Diagrams for gear-cutting machines, a kind of milling machine, were discovered in Leonardo Da Vinci's notes drawn in the sixteenth century. The understanding and the use of gears in machinery, as well as the tools to cut those gears, developed actively until the twentieth century.

Clockmakers of the seventeenth and eighteenth centuries calculated gear arrangements of clock wheels and, in doing so, influenced the French mathematician Charles Camus who worked out a systematic and general theory of the mechanisms of gears in the eighteenth century. Clock and watch producers have always been among the main users of gear-cutters, along with cotton mills, which employed extensive gear trains in their carding and spinning machinery. In the early part of the nineteenth century, it was the development of more accurate gear cutters and wheel cutters that allowed for eventual standardization and the interchangeability of watch parts, which in turn allowed Americans to pioneer the mass production of factory-made watches. As the nineteenth century progressed, new uses were found for gearing, so that by 1850 there were hundreds of mechanisms in many different industries that worked on the principle of gear trains. As gearing became increasingly sophisticated, new, specialized gear-cutter machines were developed to meet the new requirements.

The development of machinery could not have happeed without the use of wire, for it is from this metal product that screws are made. For such products as watches and clocks and other small machines, arbors and staffs that hold small gears are also made from wire. Wire drawing, the pulling of a strand of metal through a hole thus making it smaller than the heated metal rod which is its host, was first mentioned in writings from eighth century Europe. It is true that the Egyptian pharaohs wore gold wire necklaces but these were cut and hammered into a round shape. Commercial scale wire was sold in France in 1270 and in England in 1465. In 1350, the Germans began drawing wire through metal plates for use in pianos. The first wire drawing was done in America in 1775 in Norwich, Connecticut.

Until the nineteenth century, wire was drawn by hand through a die and so only short lengths could be made, but by 1830, several new types of wire drawing machines were developed. In the 1850s the industry was stimulated by new wire drawing techniques and by the surging need for bicycle spokes. By 1860, 1500 tons of wire per year were being produced for use in making women's hoop skirts. The year 1875 saw the beginning of wire drawing in the making of nails and wire rope used for making cable.

TRANSPORTATION

Change to a central factory system meant a tremendous increase in production. Having raw materials and workers all under one roof allowed for better coordination and increased efficiency within, and between, various steps on the way to a finished product. This change also created larger population centers as people moved to mill villages just outside the factory walls, much the same way that villages in medieval times grew up outside the walls of feudal castles. Subsistence farming, the livelihood of three-quarters of the population of the United States in the early nineteenth century, changed drastically to produce food for larger groups of people who did not farm. New means of transportation, canal systems, steamboats and locomotives allowed for greater movement of raw materials and manufactured goods between these industrial centers and the large shipping ports of Boston and New York. The opening of the Erie Canal in the 1820's, between New York and Lake Erie, saw a flood of farm products and then manufactured goods pour into New York City. However, even though a system of canals was built throughout the northeast and the western states of Ohio and Pennsylvania, the railroad had the advantage of being faster. Tracks could extend in more flexible routes, and could be laid more efficiently and economically than the digging of canals. Plus, shipments could be made from one center to another without as much loading and unloading. In 1834, an inventor named Ross Winans developed the *bogie*, a double axle that stabilized carriages and freight cars on American trains, allowing them to carry heavier loads and maintain longer strings of attached cars. Factory centers like those in Massachusetts, Worcester and Lowell, and later Fitchburg, became railheads. Bustling farmers' markets grew at these centers where produce, livestock, and cordwood could be sold to the local populace or shipped to other centers.

Nathaniel Hawthorne wrote in 1844, "The whistle of the locomotive tells the story of busy men." In 1840 there were 3300 miles of train tracks in the country, equal to the number of canal miles. New England had 436 miles of track. By 1850 there were 8900 miles of track in the country, of which 2633 served New England. The only section of the United States lacking the boom in railroad growth was the South, which had fifty percent less miles of track than New England in an area two-thirds larger. Throughout the 1840s the race was on to construct the railroads needed to move raw materials inland from the Boston and New York seaports and to move finished products both toward the new expansion in the west and back toward the same ports in the east for shipment to foreign markets. The Western Railroad from Boston, through Worcester to create a link to Albany, New York, a major port on the Erie Canal, opened in 1841. In 1845, Alvah Crocker, the leading industrialist of Fitchburg, headed the completion of the construction of the Boston-Fitchburg Railroad, which helped establish the town as one of many industrial centers of the United States prior to the Civil War. Throughout the middle and late nineteenth century, more than a hundred freight and passenger trains moved in and out of Fitchburg every day.

FINANCING A MOVEMENT

With the new era of industrialization came a new way of doing business. The use of paper money as currency began to replace gold specie. The ratio of paper money to specie used in 1828 was three to one, five years later it was more than eight to one. On a larger scale, with the development of new industries came the expanded use of stock companies to finance them. As Daniel Webster pointed out in 1849, "A corporation, the union of many people to form capital, is the best way of carrying on those operations which apply science to art to produce the things essential to man's existence." Since there was not a great deal of individual wealth in the early years of the new United States, an entrepreneurial effort of any size might be either financed by venture capital from London or be undertaken as a group effort, with the selling of shares in the new company. A precedent for this sharing of investment already existed much earlier in America's farm culture where, even though farms were individually owned, grist mills, saw mills and tanneries very often were established in a group effort to the advantage of all in the community. Selling public shares in a company, or to finance some particular operation, was first tried in London in 1719, by both the Bank of England and the South Seas Trading Company. The first panic and subsequent stock market crash occurred the very next year with the bursting of what was called the South Sea Bubble. From that time to the present, the formation of stock companies and the selling of shares on stock markets has progressed to the extent that the economies of countries, and lately of the entire globe, rise and fall with the health of various stock markets.

The industrial age in America can be plotted in its economic cycles of boom and bust, but always in its steady growth to make the United States one of the wealthiest countries in history. At the time of the American Revolution and the roughly forty years after the signing of the peace treaty in 1783, the economy of the new country remained fairly static. Suddenly, in the 1830s and up to 1860, the economy began to grow by roughly 2% per year. This could be attributed in a small way to advanced techniques in agricultural output, but was mostly due to the shifting from an agricultural to an industrial economy. The industrial expansion in the North led to a deeper chasm between it and the South. Indeed, the conflict between the brash new capitalistic industrial North and the older, genteel agricultural South had been brewing since the time of Jefferson's and Hamilton's differences of opinion at the turn of the century. The Industrial Revolution in the North led the United States in the direction it would eventually go and it could not wait for the much slower progress of its southern sister.

Throughout history, most people have tried for a balance between their ethics and their wallet. Abolitionists argued about the immorality of owning slaves, but an even stronger push for emancipation came from industry and commerce. The federal government in the 1850s was pushed more by private capitalist interests than by abolitionists to do away with slavery. Once the war started, and after it was over, during the reconstruction period, private business interests became the major influence on the federal government. Because of this influence it is possible to say that, until 1860 the government of the United States was mainly about ideology, and from that time on it was mostly about money. From the adoption of the Constitution to the opening salvos of the Civil War, Washington D.C. focused on how the country should be run. Once the country committed itself to actually fighting for those ideals, the next task was to figure out how to pay for them.

LABOR AND MANAGEMENT

In 1840 over 63% of America's labor force made their living on farms. Only 8% were in manufacturing, and the rest in such private enterprises as transportation, logging, mining, construction and trade. Close to 90% of the manufacturing work force was concentrated in the northeast. Along with expansion of industry and the railroads, the work force throughout the country more than doubled by 1870. By that year the number of people in manufacturing was almost 20% of the total work force, but in farming the number had dropped to 53%. This was in spite of the fact that liberated slaves, unlike before, were now counted as part of the work force, and also despite the fact that agriculture had expanded immensely in the Midwest and West. Industrial expansion grew by 500% over this period, mostly in the New England and Mid-Atlantic states.

For two hundred years prior to the American Industrial Revolution, this country's agrarian culture had fostered a society based on equality among its citizens. In contrast to the rigid social class system of England, this new egalitarian mode of living indeed became one of the major sentiments that fomented the break from the mother country. With the establishment of the factory system, however, class inequality again reared its head. Many early tinkerers and inventors, who were small capitalists, built machine shops that became factories and eventually large manufacturing plants, turning those same tinkerers into major industrial capitalists. When Samuel Slater brought over from England the new textile technology, he also brought England's labor practices to go with it. An example was the hiring of children to operate the machines for wages, as opposed to taking them on as apprentices. Under the apprentice system, a young man would be taken on by a master who would teach him all facets of his trade, whereas in the factory system, a child would be taught only that one activity, at which he would work repetitiously day after day. Beginning with Francis Cabot Lowell's mill in Waltham, women went to work away from home. Both women and children required little skill or training to run the machines in the factories. Most machines were self-acting; once they were set up, and an unskilled worker could run them.

By the middle of the nineteenth century, when people left the farms and went to work in manufacturing, they were not starting their own small businesses as they might have earlier and might do today. Only a very small group of capitalists at that time knew how to run a profitable factory business. To run a successful manufacturing company, the owner would need to know how to maintain the plant, how to hire, motivate and train groups of workers, how to transport large quantities of raw materials, store those materials and supply the machinery and line workers to keep the plant running steadily and efficiently. No schools or books existed to teach optimization, logistics or plant management. The few who knew how to run a business more than likely prospered, while the rest usually went under before they learned.

In the 1870s, a farm worker or an immigrant laborer who moved into the manufacturing sector usually went to work in a factory. He would be supervised by a skilled laborer or craftsman, who would himself be overseen by a department manager or a plant superintendent, who in turn would be hired for that position by an owner or a board of directors of the company. An unskilled laborer might become a craftsman or an owner might manage a plant, but the occupational and cultural barrier between the laborer/craftsman on one side of the social and economic divide, and the owner/manager on the other side was rarely ever breached.

INDUSTRY COMES OF AGE

America's industrial age has been replaced by the advance of the electronic/computer revolution. The technological, economic and social changes that began in the early eighteenth century and were solidified by the nineteenth century are being changed again to create the *dot com* world of today. The change now, in many ways mirrors the early social changes from farm-based society to the industrial-based one. By the late 1870s, what had been a revolution, became a way of life. By that time the change-over from an agricultural society was complete and the industrial age had reached its maturity. The Industrial Revolution had its infancy from 1800 to 1820, its childhood in the rapid growth and development of the 30s, 40s and 50s, its stormy adolescence in the 60s, finally reaching adulthood in the 70s. Industry, including manufacturing and transportation, had come of age by America's one hundredth birthday in 1876.

In that centennial year the country floundered financially in the middle of a six-year depression, the worst so far in our history. The stock market had crashed with the Panic of 1873. What began with the fall of the Berlin stock market the year before, dominoed through Vienna, Paris, Rome and London. Up to that time, a large percentage of American companies still looked to London for loans and venture financing, and with the fall of the British economy these monies all but dried up. The European crash, coinciding with over-investment in railroads and the collapse of the American banking system, combined to throw the country into a financial depression that lasted until 1879. Before the depression of the 1870s, the meteoric rise of American industry was fueled by dreams, aspirations, creativity and technological innovation. The economic constriction of the depression years affected every manufacturing industry in the country, and served to introduce the more unrealistic dreamers to the hard realities of debit and credit. From 1880 on, the success of any manufacturing firm could only be measured by its ability to translate innovation into profit and loss.

Labor strife throughout the country became rampant during the depression. By 1876, many workers' salaries were cut by up to 50% in desperate measures by factory owners to keep people on the job. Still, one of every ten factory workers in the country was let go. Thousands of tramps roamed the countryside and immigration dropped off drastically. Early that year, Massachusetts passed the country's first child labor laws forbidding manufacturing or mercantile establishments from using children under the age of ten. The Convention of Workingmen that met in Boston in October 1877 proposed that half-time schools be set up for children employed in factories. However, until the twentieth century, child labor laws were never enforced. Strange as it may seem, the 8-hour workday law for all factory workers had been in effect since 1868, and several strikes throughout the 1870s attempted to secure enforcement of the law, but to no avail. By 1880, the law was dead.

While the country was reaching its industrial maturity in the middle 1870s, initial battles for great social changes were being fought. Samuel Gompers urged all workers to unite. Before that year, only one worker in a hundred belonged to a union. In August 1876, ten Molly Maguires, Irish immigrant coal miners, were found guilty of murdering their bosses in the anthracite mines of Pennsylvania. In July of 1877, railroad workers revolted and burned the roundhouse at Pittsburg. In the same month, federal troops fired on workers of the Baltimore and Ohio Railroad in West Virginia, killing thirteen men. An article appeared in the *Fitchburg Sentinel* in May of 1877, stating that, "Within the last two weeks, no less than 200,000 people…employed upon our railroads, shops, and mines, have engaged in strikes, and have suddenly transformed themselves into the criminal classes. Since the panic of 1873, it is estimated that a million men have been thrown out of employment."

In 1876, Rutherford B. Hayes was elected President, replacing the financially scandal-ridden administration of Ulysses S. Grant. Elizabeth Cady Stanton and Susan B. Anthony presented to Congress on July 4th, 1876, the "Declaration of Rights of the Women of the United States." In that same month, the Indian wars in the West were reaching their peak with the massacre of Custer's cavalry troop on the banks of the Little Big Horn River.

The Centennial Exhibition had opened in Philadelphia in May of 1876. Ten million dollars had been raised to finance the exhibition in which thirty countries from all over the world sent contributions of money as well as their latest advances in technology. Fitchburg, Massachusetts was well represented with exhibitions of many products made in the city.

Central to the exhibit was the 1500 horsepower Corliss steam engine in Mechanics Hall, providing power for the entire exhibition. Displayed next to the Corliss, at that time the largest steam engine in the world, was the smallest steam engine in the world. This miniature machine, measuring 1/8 inch square, could be covered with a sewing thimble, and yet it had all the details of the Corliss engine, a boiler, cylinder, governor, and valves. The tiny engine had been made by a Connecticut watchmaker named D.A.A. Buck. The following year, Buck designed the first Waterbury watch, which led the way to providing the country with an inexpensively produced timepiece, affordable to the average working man.

The American Waltham Watch Company's Model 1872 pocket watch won the first prize as the best-of-show. It had achieved a status among the watchmaking industry as the best mass-produced watch in the world, and could hold its own with any of the finest watches Europe could produce. The American-manufactured pocket watch stood proud as a symbol of the American System of Manufacture.

Designed three years after the Waltham Model 1872, the Fitchburg Watch, equal in beauty, style and function, was manufactured in 1875. The machinery used to build this watch was the end result of an evolution in machine tool development from the early years of the century. The company responsible for the watch's design and manufacture was formed with the kind of knowledge that comes with trial and error experience over many years. It resulted from the same aspirations, dreams, financial investment, and hard work that typified all major industries that drove the revolution, and it suffered the same hardship of under-capitalization that the economic depression inflicted upon all the country's industries.

Peter Henlein, inventor of the first watch, circa 1509, in Nuremburg, Germany

Chapter 3

BEFORE THE FACTORIES

The Fitchburg Watch is a creation of that distinctly American phenomenon, the mass production of quality pocket watches. It was made during the height of the American Industrial Revolution, and at a time when the United States first took its place as the world leader in the manufacture of machine-made quality watches. For everyday use there was no better watch. The technology of watchmaking reached its apogee in the 1870s. Temperature insensitive materials, as well as self-winding, shockproofing, waterproofing, sweep second hands, and safety pinions, all invented and used before that time, would not be in common usage until much later. They would continue to improve on the watches' efficiency and durability, but the mass-produced watch that could be bought in the last quarter of the nineteenth century

49

would keep time as well as, or better than, any mechanical watch that came before or after it.

American mass-produced watches are often said to be machine-made, as opposed to certain European products, which are advertised as hand-made. Neither term is exactly correct. All mechanical watch parts are made with machinery, and all watches are assembled and adjusted by hand. The modern Swiss watch, like the Patek-Phillipe, which is advertised as hand-made, is manufactured basically the same way as those made by a nineteenth century watch factory. What is meant by a machine-made watch is one that contains parts which are interchangeable. The difference—which can be significant— between what is called machine-made and what is called hand-made, is the number of watches made in a given time and the degree of human involvement required for fine adjustment for temperature, positions, and isochronism.

By the middle of the twentieth century, even before the popularity of the quartz movement, it was unusual to find an American adult who did not own a watch. This democratization of portable time could only have come about through the American System of machine-made, mass-produced watch manufacture. The highly accurate, easily worn watches of the twentieth century, turned out by the thousands every day in America are a far cry from the first cumbersome, highly inaccurate watches, each painstakingly made by hand in Europe centuries ago.

FROM THE BEGINNING

Clocks appeared in Europe in the fourteenth century.

The first clocks were used in monasteries to ring bells calling the monks to prayer. The secular use for clocks was pretty much for the same reason, to call people to meetings or assemblies. With the beginning of the Industrial Revolution in Europe, clocks were being used for a different purpose, to let people know when they were supposed to be at their station and when they were to leave. With the development of the watch, an individual could carry his knowledge of time with him, and the person who controlled the use of time had power over those under him. The knowing of time came to be seen as power itself.

The direct line of evolution from the first watch to the Fitchburg Watch goes back almost five hundred years, coinciding with the beginning of two major trends that would completely change the view of the world as it was known. At the turn of the sixteenth century, Gutenburg's printing medium, which up till that time had been producing only Bibles, had started the long process of the dissemination of information to large masses of people that would eventually lead them out of the dark ages. The second major trend was begun by Christopher Columbus, who led the opening of the passage to the Americas, a process that eventually enclosed the entire planet in a global interchange of markets, races, and political philosophies.

The evolution of the portable timekeeper walked hand in hand through this same period of our history. It is interesting to note that all three of these trends, a high degree of literacy, the rise of the United States as the world leader, and widespread ownership of the watch all follow pretty much the same upward curve. There may not necessarily be a causal relationship between these three factors, but there is certainly an indicative one. Gains in literacy and globalization, as well as accuracy and mass ownership of watches made only minimal gains in the sixteenth century, rose steadily in the seventeenth, precipitously in the eighteenth, and came to maturity in the nineteenth century, all at pretty much the same rate.

Prior to the turn of the sixteenth century, early clockwatches, as they were called, were small table clocks that could be carried from one room to another. The first watch itself appeared in 1509, developed by Peter Henlein in Nuremburg, Germany. Early watches measured several inches in diameter and were drum-shaped. It was not until half a century later that watches were made small enough to be carried on one's person. The technology that allowed for this portability of time was the invention of the mainspring, a flat ribbon of steel that, when wound into a spiral, could replace the weights used to drive the time train of the clock. There were clocks that already existed using mainsprings—the earliest record of one being 1455, the same year Gutenburg produced his first printed Bible—but it took fifty years before one was developed for a watch. Throughout the sixteenth century, the only real changes in watches were the shape and size. They became more circular and were being put into smaller cases. Even though the movements were still held together for the most part by tapered pins, watchmakers had begun to utilize tiny screws, which were developed around 1550.

In the sixteenth and early seventeenth centuries, even though watches did not keep very good time, they became fashionable items for aristocratic gentlemen to wear at their waists on chatelaines. In the 1650s, during the reign of Oliver Cromwell in England, clothing styles, as dictated by Puritan beliefs, became plain to the point of austerity. Watches were made with plain silver cases in lieu of ornate gold and enamel, and were worn for the first time inside a pocket of the newly styled garments which we know as vests. Around this time they became known as pocket watches, and had become roughly the same shape they appear today.

To use the power of a wound mainspring for the approriate running of a clock or a watch it is necessary to equalize the deliverance of its energy to the mechanism over a period of time. The power of a wound spring will decline from when it is fully wound to when it is nearly unwound, causing the timepiece to run faster or slower, and thus rendering it less accurate as a timekeeper. To counteract this, so that the power is delivered evenly from one winding to the next, three major types of mechanisms have been invented. The first watches used what was called a stackfreed, developed in the 1470s. This consisted of a strong curved spring plus a cam. The stackfreed spring was curved in such a way that, when the mainspring was fully wound, it would retard the mainspring's power and, along with the cam, would augment the mainspring near the end of its run, thus evening out the power delivered.

Somewhere around 1525, a clockmaker named Jacob Czech in Prague began using what is called a fusee, which had also been developed in the 1470s. The fusee was a conical-shaped pulley upon which was wound a cat-gut cord at one end and the mainspring barrel at the other. By 1664, the cord was replaced by a miniature bicycle-like chain. The pulley itself looks somewhat like the gears on a five-speed bicycle, being progressively variable and attached to the great wheel arbor to which it transfers power. The mainspring must pull the smaller gear when it is freshly wound, moving to progressively larger gears as it winds down. The fusee allowed for a relatively better timekeeper than the stackfreed. Since the time of its first use, the fusee has always been touted as helping to provide the highest degree of accuracy in a mechanical watch. It was used until the 1880s in English-made watches and into the middle of the twentieth century in eight-day marine chronometers.

The third type of equalizing mechanism is the going barrel with the Geneva stop work. In this case, the barrel, which encases the mainspring, is attached to the great wheel. The stop work consists of two gears, one of which has one tooth and is attached to the barrel arbor. The other gear is a star wheel with five or more teeth, one tooth having a concave end with the others convex. The meshing of the two gears eliminates the outer ends of the mainspring being wound, thus preventing the mainspring from being wound too tightly to cause it to run faster, or to be wound out to its fullest thus causing it to run slower. Invented in 1776 by a French watchmaker named Jean-Antoine Lepine, the going barrel with a Geneva stop work—making use of a contemporary more resilient mainspring—was much easier to manufacture than the fusee even though it was not quite as accurate. It was immediately popular among French watchmakers as they found the trade-off between ease of manufacture and scale of accuracy to be favorable. American watchmakers, beginning in the middle of the nineteenth century, copied the French in this regard. The difference in accuracy between watches with a going barrel and those with a fusee came to be less than a minute a day.

In the latter part of the seventeenth century, even with the use of the fusee and the newly invented balance wheel developed in the early part of the century, the accuracy of the pocket watch was still notoriously bad, losing about fifteen minutes a day. Like the clock, they continued to utilize the verge escapement to control and regulate the amount of power released to operate the watch mechanism. The need for precision in a portable timepiece had begun to occupy the thinking of some of the foremost scientific minds of the day. In 1675, in what is considered by many to be the major turning point in the development of the watch, the concept of the balance spring was developed simultaneous by two different scientists.

Robert Hooke, a physicist and collaborator of Isaac Nwton, had distinguished himself in many different fields of scientific investigation. He is author of Hooke's Law of elasticity, which laid the basis for understanding the stress and strain of elastic materials, and which led ultimately to the development of the spiral balance spring. Aside from this, Hooke was known for the discovery of refraction of light rays, as the developer of the first Georgian telescope, and for his detailed illustrations of Mars and Jupiter. In another area altogether, he is also known for his investigations into the possibility of artificially manufacturing fibers, for being the first person to use the word "cell" in describing microscopic organisms, and as an early proponent of Darwinian-type evolution.

The second person to develop the balance spring as it is used today was a Dutchman named Christaan Huygens. A mathematician, astronomer, and physicist, Huygens founded the wave theory of light, which was later stated in mathematical terms by Robert Maxwell and subsequently used as a basis for Einstein's theories of relativity. In other fields, Huygens discovered the true shape of the rings of Saturn, and made many original contributions to the science of dynamics, the mathematics of curvatures, and the laws of centrifugal force. He invented the pendulum for clocks in 1656, and influenced John Harrison's later work on the measurement of longitude. Whereas Hooke's balance spring was a straight spring, Huygens developed the spiral balance spring, which immediately found wide, popular usage and became the standard for all mechanical watches.

The verge escapement was probably used in ninety-five percent of all watches made between 1509 and 1820. A few other types of escapements also found some popularity during that time. The cylinder escapement, invented by a Frenchman in 1695, was used in English watches from the middle 1700s until the 1860s, and the duplex escapement, invented by an Englishman about 1750, was popular in French watches from about 1784 until 1870. The duplex escapement was utilized again later in American "dollar watches" from the 1890s up into the twentieth century. Both the cylinder and the duplex escapements, if made extremely well, could provide a relatively high degree of accuracy.

But it was not until the improved detached lever escapement became popular in pocket watches in the 1820s that the watch evolved, from being just an aristocrat's piece of jewelry, into what could be called a precision instrument for everyday use. Invented by Thomas Mudge in England in 1750, the detached lever escapement gained popular usage after the safety action was added by Abraham Louis Breguet and others.

At the beginning of the nineteenth century, the two largest watch producing countries were England and France. The style, as well as the mechanics, of the watch made in the respective countries was different in many ways from that of the other. The English watch, copied by early American watchmakers, was large and thick. They used a fusee and mostly the verge, but sometimes a duplex escapement. They were key wound from the back, had a full plate movement—until the 1850s when they changed to mostly ¾ plates—were jeweled and had a large balance cock. They used a high domed crystal and typically spade hands, which were set from the front of the watch.

The French, on the other hand—including watchmakers in French-speaking Switzerland—produced watches that were much thinner and smaller in diameter. They used a going barrel with the Geneva stop work, and mostly verge or cylinder escapements. They wound from the front of the watch, used no jeweling, and had a bridge movement with a wedge-shaped balance cock. The crystal was flatter, and the typically moon shaped hands were set from the back.

AMERICA BEFORE THE FACTORIES

With the coming of the industrial age, the workings of a clock or watch took on a new fascination. In 1837, Edward Everett, gave a speech to the Massachusetts Charitable Mechanics Association—an organization much like the Boston Computer Club of the 1980s, made up of people fascinated with the new technology—in which he called the watch a "miracle of art" that could bring "one of the incommunicable attributes of the Deity...within the reach of man." To people new to the wonders of the mechanical age, the spirit embodied in a "few wheels and a piece of elastic steel" answered one of the most important questions one could ask on the road to eternity, "What time is it now?" In 1838, Nathaniel Hawthorne wrote that Father Time "has traded in his hour-glass for a gold patent lever watch, which he carries in his vest pocket."

The faster speeds of the railroad engine over greater distances extended the need for watches to a broader range of people. Time zones through which trains traveled from east to west were established and time checks were sent by telegraph to all the stations along the line from the central station in Boston. Regulations for railroad companies included the issuance of a good watch to "Every Conductor, Engine Driver, Switch Tender, and Bridge Tender." Henry David Thoreau wrote that he watched the passage of the "morning cars with the same feeling that I do the rising of the sun, which is hardly more regular."

The rise of the American watch industry in the second half of the nineteenth century was fueled by an increasing demand for watches. In the first half of the century, the average American did not need a watch, nor could he afford one. Individual watchmakers in the early part of the nineteenth century, men like Luther Goddard, were able to keep up with the growing demand by hand-making one watch at a time. In his entire career, Goddard turned out about 530 English-style watches with fusees and verge escapements. He learned his trade from his uncle, clockmaker Lemuel Willard, of Grafton, Massachusetts, and began production in Shrewsbury, Massachusetts in 1809, largely as a response to the embargo on British goods levied by Congress during the Jefferson administration. After the peace treaty between the Americans and the British was signed in 1814, the country became flooded with cheap English products, forcing Goddard out of business.

Jacob Custer, a clockmaker, produced about a dozen English-style watches with lever escapements between 1840 and 1845. Before the advent of mass-produced watches these men had no choice but to employ the same techniques used in European watchmaking. The Pitkin brothers, using machine tools designed to produce interchangeable watch parts, manufactured about 500 complete watches with fusees and detached lever escapements prior to 1842. They then moved to a Maiden Lane address in New York City where they made watches and watch cases until 1845. Charles Fasoldt, a German immigrant, began making watches about the same time Aaron Dennison set up the first enterprise for mass-production in 1850. But Fasoldt, who produced watches up to 1884, made fewer than 400 pieces.

Aaron Dennison, father of the American watch manufacturing industry, and Ambrose Webster, watchmaking tool designer under Dennison.

Chapter 4

AN AMERICAN WATCH FOR EVERYONE

Mass production of American watches began in 1850 in Roxbury, Massachusetts, which is now a neighborhood of Boston. Aaron Dennison, considered the father of the American watch industry, learned his trade from Jubal Howe, a former apprentice of Luther Goddard, and from European watchmakers working in New York. He studied the manufacturing methods of the Connecticut clock and weapons makers and hired a machinist named Nelson Pitkin Stratton who had apprenticed to the Pitkin brothers. Stratton had helped build the Pitkins' watch tool machinery. These relatively simple machines, the first watchmaking machines built in America, served as models for later, much more complex, machines to come after them.

Dennison and his partner, Edward Howard, established the American Horologue Company to make

English-style watches, as they were more popular than those made by the French or the Swiss. Struggling with bankruptcy in its first years of existence, the company reformed as the Warren Manufacturing Company, and later the Boston Watch Company. In 1854 they moved to Waltham, Massachusetts just a quarter mile up and across the Charles River from where Francis Cabot Lowell had located his first textile mill. Machinists Ambrose Webster and Charles Moseley joined the company and, while in its employ, developed what was to later become the standard machine tools used in many different American industries.

Before the move to Waltham, the company had made some alterations in their English-style watches. One of the more important divergences from English construction was the use of the going barrel in place of the fusee. New improvements in designs and compositions of both the main spring and the balance spring allowed for the use of the going barrel with the Geneva stop, which was much easier to construct, and had fewer parts. Unlike the British, who built their watches with the fusee until the end of the nineteenth century, the Americans never used it in any of their machine-made watches. Although, they were used later, in the twentieth century in Hamilton chronometers.

The granddaddy of all America's watch manufacturing companies, Dennison's entrepreneurial effort—later made financially successful by Royal Robbins—eventually became the American Waltham Watch Company, which, throughout its hundred year history, grew to become a major contributor in watch production throughout the world. Some later watch companies in the United States grew larger than Waltham, some lasted longer, some made a line of top quality watches that equaled or bettered

Waltham's. Many companies certainly made poorer or cheaper watches, many lived and died during Waltham's tenure, but the company built on the banks of the Charles River both pioneered and set the standard for the entire industry. The entrepreneurs of all the early watch companies that followed them either got their start at Waltham or received help from former Waltham employees. Supervisors, managers, watchmakers, machine tool designers and builders as well, moved out from employment at the Waltham company to help establish the new companies. Unlike the rigid British system of guarding technological secrets, American innovative machinists spread their seed throughout the Northeast, to the Midwest and finally to the West Coast.

From the beginning, Aaron Dennison wanted to make a medium priced watch. His intent was to fill the demands of a growing population. The company's early existence was rocky in the extreme, with five company name changes and as many financial reorganizations in the first ten years. By 1854, they were turning out ten watches a day. During the recession that followed the Panic of 1857, Robbins cut wages and copied the Lowell textile mills by hiring women to run the machines. He retooled in an effort to make a more affordable watch. Again in 1862, Dennison lobbied his bosses to make a less expensive timepiece. The trend established from the beginning in Waltham was to make a watch available to a large number of people, as opposed to the finer quality watch designed for the wealthier customer.

The first two new entrepreneurial efforts that sprang from the original company bucked this mid-priced watch trend. After the re-organization of 1857, Charles Rice, who held a mortgage on the company's holdings, removed much of the equipment, returning it to the old plant in Roxbury. He brought with him Edward Howard, as plant superintendent, as well as fifteen workmen to establish the Howard and Rice Company. This later became the E. Howard & Co. and then the Howard Watch and Clock Company. They manufactured quality watches in Roxbury until the late 1890s. The company's interest was not so much in turning out large quantities of watches as it was in making a quality timepiece, and they produced only a total of 109,650 watches from 1858 to 1895. That would average out to a little less than sixty watches per week. Unlike the Waltham company, which strove to complete by machine each function of watchmaking—except for assembly and escapement adjustment—the Roxbury company felt that a combination of machine and hand work was needed for a better watch.

The other early breakaway, not as successful, was the Nashua Watch Company. B.D. Bingham, a New Hampshire clockmaker, went to work for Dennison in the late 1850s to learn watchmaking. In 1860, he and Nelson Stratton left the company, taking with them many of American Watch Company's better machine technicians, including Charles Moseley and James Gerry, to establish a small watch manufacturing shop in Nashua, New Hampshire. They attempted to manufacture a fine precision watch. After making one model watch, they measured all the parts carefully and then built machinery that could duplicate those parts. They assembled a workforce of thirty-five people and produced enough material to make a thousand watches. Two years later they were out of money and could not find anyone to back them. They were absorbed by the American Watch Company, made a special department in the Waltham factory, and allowed to continue their efforts to produce a high quality line of precision watches.

It was largely through the efforts of the Nashua department that the watches on display at the Philadelphia Centennial Exposition in 1876 gave the European watchmakers such a shock on seeing how far the American watch industry had outdistanced them. Even more shocking than the watch itself, the Europeans were amazed by the automated machinery for making the watches on display, in particular Charles Vander Woerd's screwmaking machine, developed for the Waltham company, which could turn out 50,000 screws a day. The American Waltham Watch Company's Model 72, which won the prize at the 1876 Centennial Exposition went on to win prizes in Paris in 1878, Sidney, Australia in 1879, Melbourne in 1980, and London in 1885.

1860s THE SECOND WAVE

The war years saw a major change in the attitudes of those people who sold watches in the United States, the large jewelry dealers. With the absorbtion of the Nashua company by the American Watch Company, there were only two companies making watches in 1862. The Howard company turned out watches beyond what most people could afford. The American Watch Company (Waltham), on the other hand, experienced boom times, even paying yearly dividends on money invested. To their more affordable watch lines they added the Soldier's Watch (7 jewel, Model 57, William Ellery), carried by an increasing number of Union officers. Using a watch was considered unnecessary for enlisted men. But even with the American Waltham Company's marketing and new production efforts, their output continued to be far less than the number of European imports sold.

In 1862, Congress levied heavy tariffs on imported manufactured goods to help pay for the war effort. These tariffs were increased substantially in 1864 as the war dragged on and sucked up greater percentages of the national income. In Lincoln's inflation economy, real wages actually dropped during the war. Fewer people could afford the kind of watch most jewelers were selling at a time when import tariffs were driving prices even higher for watches coming from overseas. It seems that, almost simultaneously, several large jewelry stores and jewelry wholesalers in Boston, New York and Chicago woke up to the same idea—why don't we make our own watches? They had only to look to Waltham to see profits being made and dividends being paid, as opposed to sending dollars for products overseas and paying exorbitant tariffs to boot. Not only did the American Watch Company serve as a role model for a successful watchmaking venture, but they also contained a wellspring of know-how just waiting to be tapped.

In 1864, at least six different watchmaking companies were formed, all with the financial backing of large jewelry stores or wholesalers. These companies met with a widely varying range of success. On the one end, the National Watch Company of Illinois went on to enjoy many successful decades as the Elgin Watch Company. At the other end, there was the Union Watch Company of Boston, which dissolved only eight months after its incorporation.

All of these ventures are recorded as having their beginnngs in 1864. The National Watch Company owed their success to producing middle range and good quality timepieces up into the 1960s. In fact, according to some watch experts, the Elgin 21-jewel 16-size Interchangeable (Models 76 and 91), of which approximately a thousand were made, is the finest mass-produced, but hand-assembled, watch ever sold in America.

In the spring of 1864, John C. Adams of Chicago, head of the watch department of W.H. & C. Miller jewelry firm, and Ira Blake of the American Watch Company, who had also been part of the Nashua Watch Company venture, put together plans for a factory in Elgin, Illinois. They managed to attract other investors including the former mayor of Chicago, and the family that owned the Borden Milk Company. The citizens of Elgin donated land on which to build a factory. To design and build machinery, they lured Charles Moseley as well as several other top-notch machinists from Waltham. The power to the plant was provided by two automatic eighty horse-power steam engines, designed and built by C.H. Brown and Company of Fitchburg, Massachusetts.

With Daniel Currier, Moseley constructed the first model watch for the Elgin company. Building of the machine tools took two years and seven months and no watches were completed until 1867. The first timepieces which were made made closely resembled those from the American Watch Company. However, with improvements in design and with skillful management techniques, by the turn of the century, Elgin tied Waltham in total production and yearly output. In the twentieth century the company went on to outproduce Waltham. With the Interchangeable and the B.W. Raymond 15-jewel 18-size model, they showed they could turn out a top-of-the-line precision watch, but like the American Watch Company, they made their fortune on the design and manufacture of a dependable mid-range watch for everyday use.

The first five directors of the Elgin company were not expert at watchmaking, they were managers and business men who knew how to hire the expertise that was needed. As with the managerial and financial expertise of Royal Robbins at Waltham, those at Elgin found the working balance between capitalist and craftsman.

It is possible that part of Elgin's success may have been due, at least in the early years just after the war, to their distance from Waltham's coercive marketing techniques. In the same way it was easier for jewelers in Boston and New York to buy from a domestic source rather than import from Europe, it was certainly easier for those in midwestern cities to buy from the Chicago area. For those jewelers in Massachusetts and New York, however, the American Watch Company was able to exert a great deal of pressure in keeping Elgin from getting a proper foothold. It is possible that this kind of pressure is what kept the jewelry firm of Palmers and Batchelders in Boston from getting the Union Watch Company of Boston off the ground. They took out incorporation papers in the fall of 1864 only to dissolve the corporation in the spring of 1865 with nothing to show for their effort. They had, prior to this time, been an important outlet for American Watch Company's products, buying movements to put in cases they had made elsewhere. It would not have been difficult for the American Watch Company to merely choke off their supply at the first hint of unwanted competition.

A second Boston venture of this period fared somewhat better than the Union Watch Company of Boston. It involved a collaboration between Aaron Dennison,

American Watch Company's original founder, and A.O. Bigelow of the Bigelow, Kennard & Company jewelry firm. In 1864, they formed the Tremont Watch Company in Boston. Dennison, ever the innovator, came up with the idea of manufacturing the more delicate parts, such as gear trains, escapements, and balances, in Switzerland and shipping them to the Boston plant for assembly. The larger, more easily manufactured parts, like top plates, were made in the Tremont Street plant. B.D. Bingham, one of the founders of the Nashua Watch Company, was hired as superintendent of the Boston plant. Without the expense of time and money needed for building watch machinery, they began turning out watches within the year.

Dennison's idea made Tremont Watch Company an almost immediate success. The watches were of good quality, with parts being made inexpensively by cheap Swiss labor. High tariffs were avoided because they were not imported as assembled watches. Money was invested in a factory in Melrose, Massachusetts, a suburb of Boston, where Bigelow owned land. In their second year of production, they decided to consolidate the whole operation with the Swiss and the Boston product lines under one roof. They renamed this amended venture the Melrose Watch Company. Dennison argued with his partners, saying that making all the parts in Boston was not a good idea. And it turned out he was right. The plan proved the company's undoing. To finish the construction of the plant, as well as building the machinery for making delicate watch parts, took time and money, and, as companies before and after them had found out, they went broke before they could turn out a proper line of watches. By 1868, their capital spent and no investors in sight, they closed their doors. What machinery they owned was sold to a British company. Aaron Dennison, who had left the company as a result of his quarrel with them over production methods, accompanied the machinery to England where he eventually prospered, making watch cases.

Of the three companies started in 1864 with New York jewelry money, the one that could probably be considered the most successful was the New York Watch Company, later the New York Manufacturing Company, then the Hampden Watch Company, and finally called the Dueber-Hampden Watch Company in 1923. This enterprise was originally located in Providence, Rhode Island, but called the New York Watch Company for the people putting up the money. An Italian immigrant named Don Mozart set the factory up to manufacture a European-style watch, modified to use a three-gear train. Two and one-half years later, the financial backers brought in L.W. Cushing, from the American Watch Company, to reorganize. Mozart left and went to Michigan to eventually set up another watch factory, and the New York Watch Company moved to Springfield, Massachusetts. They brought in James Gerry from United States Watch Company of Marion, New Jersey, another 1864 start-up. Gerry originally came from the American Watch Company and the old Nashua Watch Company. They also brought in several other machinists who had worked for the American Waltham Company. The plant in Springfield was partially destroyed by fire in 1870 but they recovered, and by 1880 were the third largest producer in the country behind Waltham and Elgin. They moved to Ohio in 1889, merging with the Dueber Watch Case Company. In 1930 the company was sold to Russia.

The center of the jewelry district in New York City in the mid-nineteenth century was a street in lower Manhattan called Maiden Lane. Two of the shrewder businessmen of Maiden Lane were Louis Fellows and Robert Schell who, in 1850, had invested in Aaron Dennison's new company and obtained exclusive rights to sell the Boston Watch Company's products in the city. Some movements had been engraved Fellows and Schell during the period of time the company had been called the Warren Manufacturing Company. Fellows and Schell also sold Howard watches. In 1864, when they were ready to start making watches on their own, they hired Napoleon Sherwood, who had been with the Boston Watch Company and who later designed machinery for E. Howard & Co. Two years after setting up the watch company in New York, Fellows died. Sherwood had left, and the company, which was now officially called Robert Schell & Company, moved across the Hudson River to Newark, New Jersey. By 1867 they were selling key-wound watches as well as a newly patented stem-winding watch. The company engraved the words "Newark Watch Company" or "Newark Watch Works" on their movements, even though the company was always officially called Robert Schell & Company. Some stem-wound watches were also marked "Keyless Watch Company." The early stemwinders were difficult to make and did not hold up well, so the company eventually went back to making only key-wind movements, many of which were marked with the names of jewelers who retailed them in their own cases. The company was never really profitable and was sold in 1869 to Paul Cornell, who, with the help of John C. Adams, late of the Elgin National Watch Company, moved the operation to the

Chicago area and set it up as the Cornell Watch Company. Five years later, still not making a profit, they moved to California where they could hire Chinese workers for small wages. But that venture also fell through. The company's regular Caucasian workers went on strike, which, while not exactly causing the company to shut down during January in the depression year of 1876, helped it along. Three months later, they re-opened in Berkeley, California, with the citizens of that community, like those of Elgin, donating land for the factory. This new venture, The California Watch Company, lasted only a few months, and the machinery was then sold to the Independent Watch Company of Fredonia, New York.

Last, but certainly not least, of the 1864 companies was the United States Watch Company. This effort was begun by another Maiden Lane jewelry firm, Giles, Wales & Company. They formed a stock company, constructed a new factory in the Marion section of Jersey City, New Jersey and hired James Gerry from Waltham to design and build their machinery. Frederick Giles came originally from Montague, Massachusetts and, even though his and Wales's jewelry business was based in New York City, many of his business ties were still in the area where he came of age. The Putnam Machine Company of Fitchburg, Massachusetts designed and constructed the new factory's steam plant. The first superintendent was Frederick Giles' cousin, William Learned. One of Learned's good friends was a watchmaker from Fitchburg named Henry J. Lowe, whom he hired to be the finish room supervisor, and who later succeeded him as one of the company's superintendents. Another Fitchburg man by the name of Sylvanus Sawyer invested money in the

Marion venture and eventually became one of the major stockholders in the company.

By 1867, the United States Watch Company was turning out a line of quality watches. Their new stemwinders were better than Newark's and predated Waltham's first stemwinders by a year. They also pioneered the use of nickel-plating and damaskeening. The company manufactured about 250,000 watches between 1867 and 1874 when they filed for bankruptcy for the third and final time. Their watches were beautiful pieces of workmanship, fine jewelry as well as good timekeepers, with the higher grades priced well above any other watch on the market. Some experts consider the "United States Watch Company" grade 16-size, ¼ plate and bridge, 19-jewel movement to be the finest watch produced in America at that time.

The company, however, experienced great difficulty standing up against the competition of the American Waltham Watch Company, who had learned by this time how to produce a mid-range timepiece just as good as United States Watch Company's for less money. Plagued with slack sales, and under-capitalization, the United States Watch Company also suffered from labor problems. They experienced a large turn over in their work force, with workers leaving en masse on two separate occasions. When William Learned was ousted from his position as superintendent he instituted a lawsuit that he eventually won in a labor relations court two years later. The company went through financial reorganization is 1869 and again in 1872 when they closed and opened again under the name of Marion Watch Company. Three years later, during the depression year of 1874, they closed for good. They were able to sell some of their machinery to what would become the Independent Watch Company of Fredonia, New York. They sold other machinery to what would become the Auburndale Watch Company of Massachusetts, and still other machinery was taken by stockholder Sylvanus Sawyer to help cover a part of the loss of his financial investment. Sawyer, probably with help from Henry J. Lowe, negotiated for himself the acquisition of Marion's best equipment, the machinery used in making their high-quality and their medium grade 16-size, ¼ plate and bridge movements. With a remaining inventory of stock and what little equipment remained, Marion reorganized a new venture called the Empire Watch Company and then limped along until 1877 when that effort too was abandoned.

1870s THE SHAKE-OUT

Originally organized in 1869 by John C. Adams, the Illinois Springfield Watch Company began work on building machinery in April of 1870. There are some interesting parallels between this company and that of the Fitchburg company. First, both company's origins shared something in common. Adams went before the Springfield Board of Trade for the purpose of interesting the citizens in this new venture of establishing a watch factory in their city. His argument, much like Sylvanus Sawyer's six years later to the Fitchburg Board of Trade, was that such an enterprise would be a great boon to the community, in that it was labor intensive, providing jobs for the town, without the necessity of having to move a great deal of raw material in or finished product out. As in Fitchburg years later, the industrial leaders of Springfield decided in favor of it. However, unlike Fitchburg, the Illinois Springfield Watch Company went on to wonderful success, becoming, in the twentieth century, the country's third largest producer—behind Elgin and Waltham—of conventional-jeweled watches, including a line of first-rate railroad watches. In 1927, they merged with the Hamilton Watch Company.

An interesting note on the success of this company is that they were not able to show a profit until the year 1879, a good ten years after the idea was first proposed. The money raised among the citizens of Springfield for the stock company was enough to carry it through almost two years of the plant construction and machine tool building phase. They began producing watches in 1872 but found difficulty in selling them. In 1873, the same year as the panic that began the depression, they had expanded their facilities and opened a sales office on Maiden Lane in New York City. By 1875, sales were so slow that, even though they could have avoided bankruptcy, they had no funds to continue production. Again supported by the citizens of Springfield and the company employees, who accepted company scrip for their wages, they reorganized the stock company and struggled on until the depression finally lifted in 1879.

In 1874 there were five viable watch companies in existence in America that were destined to last throughout the depression. Waltham was turning out about 100,000 watches a year, Elgin about 40,000. Howard and New York/Hampden were each making about 1,200 a year, as was Illinois Springfield Watch Company. In 1874, the first full year of the depression, Marion went under. Two years later the Cornell/ California Watch Company was gone. Don Mozart's venture in Michigan, where he'd moved after Providence, had been short lived. His equipment was bought by the Rock Island Watch Company, which tried to set up business in Illinois in 1871 and failed. The machinery then went to the Freeport Watch Company, also in Illinois, which incorporated in 1875, but was wiped out by fire of suspicious origins later that year, and never re-opened. In addition to these larger companies, there were about five small, individual watchmakers each turning out from five to thirty watches a year.

John C. Adams of Chicago, who was instrumental in setting up the Elgin National Watch Company, became known as the "Great Starter." When Elgin was on its feet and running, Adams pulled out their top engineers and helped set up the Illinois Springfield Watch Company. The following year saw him buying up equipment from the defunct Newark Watch Company and setting up the Cornell Watch Company in Illinois. When Cornell moved to California, Adams organized the short-lived Adams & Perry Watch Company, which sold out after a few years to the Lancaster Watch Company of Pennsylvania. The Lancaster company struggled through the depression with citizens of the town of Lancaster in 1878, the last year of the depression raising money to keep the factory open. They finally closed in 1890, selling their equipment to the Hamilton Watch Company. Adams showed up again in the 1880s in the organization of the Peoria Watch Company, who made railroad watches for about ten years with equipment from the defunct Fredonia Watch Company.

The years 1874 and 1875 saw a small flurry of start-up watch companies. Only one survived for any length of time, the Rockford Watch Company, which made railroad watches and medium grade watches for everyday use.

Rockford's success, which lasted until the early part of the twentieth century, was due mostly to the fact that they concentrated on the railroad watch, a good solid, functional timepiece, not very fancy, but bought and carried by thousands of railroad men across the country.

Of the other companies originated in 1874, two involved somewhat radically new movement designs, neither of which proved to be practical. In Washington, D.C., Jason Hopkins lasted less than a year. And the Freeport Watch Company of Illinois set up their equipment to facilitate a design by C.H. Hoyt's, before they were burnt out without having turned out a single watch.

It was also in 1875 that Sylvanus Sawyer, under the auspices of the Fitchburg Board of Trade, started the watch company in that city. With his acquisition of the United States/Marion Watch Company's machinery and the hiring of their superintendent and several mechanics, he brought to Fitchburg all that was needed to manufacture and mass-produce a top grade watch. This specimen was the culmination of machine tool technology, as well as watch manufacturing design and materials composition that had evolved over the past twenty-five years beginning with Aaron Dennison and Charles Fasoldt in 1850. Manufactured like any other mass-produced watch of its time, the single Fitchburg Watch was made with United States Watch Company machinery, and undoubtedly with a few already finished parts, like a gear or an arbor, brought from New Jersey. It rivaled, in both beauty and function, the best products that Elgin or Waltham could turn out.

Sawyer was a man much like John C. Adams in entrepreneurial spirit. Though, while Adams seems to have started only watch companies, Sawyer started companies that made such products as cannons, sewing machines, and machine tools, as well as companies that performed such operations as rattan cutting and the growing of hybrid plants. Both these men set a pattern throughout their careers of starting up companies and leaving the long-term work to others.

The only other watch company that could be considered as having started in the 1870s is the Columbus Watch Company in Ohio. Began in 1876 under the name of Gruen and Savage, the company imported partly finished ebauches from Switzerland, assembled and adjusted them and fitted them into American cases. They did not, however, begin making their own movements until 1883. Dietrich Gruen eventually went on, with his son, to form the Gruen Watch Company in Cincinnati where, until 1955, he returned to the practice of importing Swiss movements for American cases.

1880s A WATCH FOR THE MASSES

An interesting socio-economic parallel can be seen between watch production in America in the later part of nineteenth century and computer production in the later part of twentieth century. From the ENIAC of the 1940s to the multi-gigabyte personal computers of the 1990s, one thrust of computer technology has been to make each successive line of computers less expensive and more available for broad consumption. In much the same way, from Aaron Dennison's original attempts to mass-produce pocket watches in the 1850s to Timex's retail sales of wrist watches in drugstores a hundred years later, a major trend of watch manufacturing has been to put a less expensive watch in the hands of more people. Even though many companies such as Waltham and Elgin maintained a high quality line of expensive watches, long-term profits were made turning out relatively inexpensive and mid-range timepieces.

Efforts had been made as far back as 1853 by the Boston Watch Company to make an inexpensive watch. George Roskopf in Switzerland had been making low-priced watches with a pin pallet escapement. Elgin and Waltham both marketed a full-plate inexpensive model. Two people who tried to take advantage of this trend were Jason Hopkins the watchmaker from Washington, D.C. and William Wales, a former owner, with Frederick Giles, of the United States/Marion Watch Company. With machinery from the bankrupt Marion company, Hopkins and Wales organized the Auburndale Watch Company in Weston, Massachsetts, practically in Waltham's back yard. The superintendent they hired died in 1876 and he was succeeded by James Gerry who had been associated previously with Waltham and with United States Watch of Marion. In 1877, Gerry left and was succeeded by William Guest who had previously moved from the watch company in Fitchburg where he had gone when the Marion company went under. Plant manager was a Chauncey Hartwell who had come from the Waltham Watch Company. By 1876, Auburndale was ready to produce an inexpensive watch, but their Hopkins rotary movement did not work as well as they had hoped, leaving them unable to produce and sell a watch inexpensively and still make a profit. They struggled along until 1883 before finally giving up and closing their doors.

But the idea of an inexpensive watch for the averag man had caught hold. The idea of what came to be called the *dollar watch* was finally realized by a Waterbury, Connecticut clock manufacturer. By the time the depression lifted in 1878, the Waterbury Watch Company, using a design by D. A. A. Buck, was turning out 150 dollar watches a day. Suddenly, in the 1880's, the ownership of a pocket watch was a goal the common man could achieve. Horatio Alger, in his inspirational stories for young boys, held up the ownership of a pocket watch as the symbolic reward for a boy who had made good. Watch clubs were formed, in which a group of factory laborers pooled their limited resources and at the end of each week drew straws, the winner buying a watch with the accumulated money. In the Waterbury Watch Company's advertisements, they stated that their watch "teaches a useful lesson, by always being regular and trustworthy" and "helps children to be punctual and prompt." Henry Ford stated that he could mass-produce a watch for as little as thirty cents apiece and years later was heard to say that he had made a big mistake not to have done so. Richard Sears, a railroad agent in Minnesota, bought an unwanted shipment of inexpensive watches and resold them individually for just a little above cost to other agents down the line. This was the first of such transactions for what would become Sears, Roebuck and Company.

From 1890 to 1930, companies like New Haven Clock Company, Ingersoll, Westclox, and Ansonia turned out an estimated total of 186 million inexpensive dollar watches. In 1930, there were a total of eleven profitable watch manufacturers in the country, with other companies like Illinois, Hampden, Rockford, and Seth Thomas having come and gone. Of the eleven surviving companies, five made mid-range to high quality watches and six made only dollar watches. The old giants like Waltham and Elgin had their inexpensive lines, but their market was completely different than that of the dollar watch companies.

The total estimated output of watches manufactured in the United States from 1890 to 1930 is about 272.6 million. Over 70% were either dollar watches or inexpensively jeweled ones. This trend continued after the interruption of the depression of the 1930s and World War II, so that by the late 1940s there would truly be available an American watch for everyone.

From the beginning of America's watch manufacturing history, the trend seems to have always been in the direction of producing a less expensive time piece that would be available to more people. Only those companies who have worked in that direction have been able to maintain any degree of long-standing financial stability. Companies like Waltham, Elgin, and Hamilton have always produced a higher quality line of watches as more of a sideline and a marketing image enhancement than with an eye toward making a decent profit on that line.

The American watch industry in the nineteenth century mirrored many other industries that measured success in terms of profitability. Long-term success was to be found in the ability to provide as many people as possible with their product. In this way, the mass-produced watch, like Henry Ford's mass-produced automobile, contributed to a large degree in the democratization of the American people.

Front and back view of a watch paper from the shop of Henry J. Lowe, showing that it was cleaned and repaired on February 2, 1848, at a cost of 75 cents.

Henry J. Lowe's shop on Main and Central Streets in 1864.

Chapter 5

AN INDUSTRIAL CENTER CARVED
FROM THE WILDERNESS

All that was generally known about the watch company of Fitchburg, prior to Fred Selchow's further fact-finding in 1968, were short entries in Charles Crossman's and Henry Abbot's books. Other mentions have been made of the company but all were based on these two sources. To verify Crossman's and Abbot's information, Selchow went to what records he could find at the Fitchburg City Hall, the town library, and the Fitchburg Historical Society. There is no record anywhere of either a Fitchburg Watch Company or a Union Watch Company having existed in the city. But Selchow did come up with a very creative piece of research. In most libraries are old directories listing everyone who lived within the city limits, their occupation, and whether they owned the house, rented it, or boarded there. In the 1876 Fitchburg street directory are five names and addresses for people whose occupations are listed as working in a watch factory. All five of these names were also listed by Charles Crossman as watchmakers who left Marion, New Jersey to come to Fitchburg. So, even though no record has ever been found of the company's incorporation or even registration in any local records, the street directory corroborates Crossman's information.

Crossman states that the company was started by Sylvanus Sawyer with Henry J. Lowe as superintendent. This is true as far as it goes. The original impetus for the commencement of this venture, and another unrelated factory at the same time, came from the newly-formed Fitchburg Board of Trade. It is true that Sawyer invested heavily in the new company, along with Thomas Palmer, also of Fitchburg and head of the board's Special Committee on the Watch Manufactory. But the Board of Trade appointed Sawyer to the directorship of the company and also appointed Henry J. Lowe to be superintendent, most probably at Sawyer's urging.

So, among the cast of characters involved in the starting of the watch company, one of the most important is the city of Fitchburg itself. The board of trade had as its purpose the stimulation of economic trade and was begun in 1874 as a response to the economic depression that gripped the country beginning with what was called The Panic of 1873. New companies were sponsored and started by the board to bring in new industry and expand employment opportunities for the residents of the city. It was this entrepreneurial spirit that had helped establish Fitchburg as one of America's first industrial cities in the early part of the nineteenth century and then inspired its growth up into the twentieth century.

The city lies approximately forty miles west of Boston in Worcester County, just a few miles from the New Hampshire border. At present, it has a population of roughly 42,000 people and is often linked with its sister city, Leominster, which is just slightly smaller in both area and population. Fitchburg's residential and industrial area began and grew populated in the valley along both sides of the Nashua River. However, the much larger land area inside the city limits extends to the hills on both sides of the river and is today thinly populated and covered by dense second-growth forest.

Fitchburg is still primarily an industrial city, even though the manufacturing plants are much smaller than in the nineteenth century and much more diversified. The last large manufacturing giant with a plant in the city, General Electric, situated for many years on the site of the old Putnam Machine Company, closed its doors in the year 2000. Most of the old nineteenth-century mill buildings have been torn down, leaving empty lots, or if still standing, are used as warehouses and offices. Many of the old nineteenth-century houses have been restored and made into modern homes that retain the character of the times they were built. Like most of America, though, shopping has moved, for the most part, from Main Street to malls on the outer edges of the city. Commuter trains come and go every day to carry people to and from high-tech workplaces in cities like Waltham and Boston. The descendants of the successive waves of immigration, English, Irish, French Canadian, Polish, Greek, Italian, and Scandinavian, have intermarried and interspersed throughout the city so that old neighborhoods like Greektown are ethnic in name only.

At the time the watch company was started, in 1875, as Fitchburg reached both a cultural and industrial peak, it was a far different place than the small, bucolic farm community that sent two companies of Minute Men to Concord a hundred years before, in 1775. In the late nineteenth century, paper mills, textile mills, furniture factories, iron foundries, and machine tool factories lined both sides of the Nashua River. Smokestacks, belching exhaust from coal-fired steam engines, crowded against the church steeples on the city's skyline. Row houses of laborer families, shanty towns of newly-arrived immigrants, and neighborhoods of rooming houses for single workingmen filled the streets between the factories. Ascending the hills, away from the river and the factories, were the more comfortable homes of the managers and, still higher up, the progressively larger homes of the owners. Sixteen blocks of Main Street, running uphill from the fork of Summer and Lunenburg Streets to Mechanic Street at the Upper Common, teemed with the daily commerce of markets, shops, banks, saloons, livery stables, hotels and churches. From the granite-block train depot, over one hundred passenger and freight trains each day ran east to Boston, west to Albany, north to New Hampshire, Vermont and Montreal, and south to Worcester, then Connecticut and New York City.

THE EARLY YEARS

It took a little over 100 years for Fitchburg to grow from a frontier outpost to a small farming town, and then to a thickly concentrated manufacturing center. The town actually began its existence as part of Lunenburg, a small village on a hill directly to the east. In 1739 John Fitch established an inn on a hill above the Nashua River in an area that was later partitioned off to become part of the town of Ashby directly to the north. He was forty years old at the time and married to Susannah Gates. Fitch had come up from Billerica, responding to the call from the Massachusetts Bay Colony for volunteers to establish outposts on what was known as the Mohawk Trail, used first by Indians and then by colonial travelers crossing the wilderness between the eastern settlements and those further west along the Connecticut River. A descendant of Zachary Fitch of Hertfordshire in England, Fitch could count among his antecedents Alfred Lord Tennyson. Within his extended family were the original British governors of India and Burma, and James Fitch, one of the founders of Yale University. A nephew was Col. Thomas Fitch, hero at Bunker Hill, and the person about whom the song Yankee Doodle Dandy was written. Fitch's namesake, his nephew John Fitch of Windsor, Connecticut received several patents for his invention of the first steamboat.

In 1744, with the beginning of the French and Indian Wars, John Fitch's inn was turned into a garrison to afford protection to settlers from Indians who, aligned with the French, swept down from Canada to prey upon British colonists. The garrison was itself overrun by a party of Abnaki Indians and French soldiers. John and Susannah, with their children, Catherine, 16; John, 12; Paul, 6; Jacob, 4; and little Susannah, 16 months, were taken prisoner and transported to Canada where they remained until their release eight years later. Susannah died on the trip home from Canada as a result of an illness that overcame her during their captivity. John, with his three sons and two daughters, returned to what was left of their homestead. They were destitute. The Abnaki had burned their house in the raid years before and the rest of the neglected property lay in ruins. Fitch petitioned the General Court of Massachusetts for money and tools. Based on his service as a provider of an outpost for the protection of travelers, the General Court allotted him enough to begin rebuilding his farm. With the help of his children and his second wife, Elizabeth Browers of Groton, Fitch rebuilt the home and established a farm. In 1764, when their small community separated from Lunenburg and incorporated as a town, the founders named the town after this hero of the French and Indian Wars. At the time of incorporation as a town, there were forty-four families within its boundaries, all subsisting on their own farms.

INDUSTRIAL GROWTH

Like most small New England communities, the first industry in the town besides farming was a grist mill. Using technology brought over from England, farmers brought their crops of corn or rye to be ground into flour. After picking a narrow spot on the Nashua River, at what is today the very heart of downtown Fitchburg, Amos and Ephraim Kimball constructed a log dam on an angle to the flow of water to deflect the swift current and produce the right amount of power to their "undershot" mill wheel. The wheel turned a stone called a "runner" that ground the meal between itself and another stationary stone called a "bedder". Each time the log dam washed away in a spring freshet, the Kimballs rebuilt it until such time as they could finally construct one of stone.

Using what was called a "flutter wheel," the Kimballs later built a sawmill with a blade imported from England. The blade, anchored between two boards, moved vertically up and down on the same principle as today's jigsaw. At approximately 120 strokes a minute, the mill could turn out between 500 and 1000 board feet a day of pine, spruce, oak or chestnut. It was in the development of sawmill technology that the early New Englanders first gained their reputation as ingenious Yankees. Until the use of steam power rendered the water wheel obsolete, the Yankee sawyer continued his quest to find new combinations of gears and wheels that would allow him a faster and stronger cut. The water turbine was developed as an improvement over the wheel and had gained in popularity before the coming of the steam engine. It had twice the efficiency of the wheel, and is still used today in different industries to generate electricity for a single plant. Examples can still be seen at locations on the Nashua River, such as the James River Paper Company plant in Pepperell, Massachusetts.

Feeding the headwater of the Nashua River, within the southwestern city limits of Fitchburg, are no less than eight streams that drain from both Mt. Wachusett to the south and Mt. Watatic to the northwest. The eastern slopes of these two small mountains on the edge of the Berkshires drain toward the New England coast. From their western slopes and beyond, the mountains drain to the Connecticut River. The Nashua flows north and then turns in a wide oxbow to flow south through Leominster and Lancaster and then sharply north again, meandering through the Nashoba Valley and finally joining the Merrimac River twenty-six miles away in Nashua, New Hampshire. In the seven miles that the river flows within

91

the city limits of Fitchburg, it drops 300 feet. Its narrow banks form a natural flume that provided the new mills with a tremendous amount of energy. With the power of this geologically ancient river, small factories were added to the sawmills and grist mills of the farmers. The same power was still used as the factories grew larger, and because rivers like the Nashua could deliver consistent year-round energy, steam power came later to New England than it did to other parts of the country.

In the latter decade of the eighteenth century, once the break with England, the post-Revolutionary War financial depression, and Shay's Rebellion were past, the new country got down to the business of building a nation. In the northern states that meant building an industrial nation. The next generation of Kimballs in Fitchburg carried on the family tradition by building a second dam upriver of the first one. Ephraim, Jr. invented a water-powered wool shearing machine to use in his new mill that also shrunk and thickened the wool—called fulling—and also cleansed, disentangled and collected the fibers—called carding. Upon the success of this venture, he later built a clothier mill. A Captain William Brown, veteran of the Revolutionary War, opened another clothier mill downriver of Kimball's original dam.

In 1796, John and Joseph Farwell built a trip-hammer mill and opened a scythe factory that began a major saw manufacturing industry in the community. Their fourteen-year-old apprentice was a boy named Asa Thurston, later destined for the missionary work in Hawaii that helped open the settlement of those islands by the United States. Asa Thurston was in recent times made famous as the hero of James Michener's book *Hawaii*, and was played by Max Van Sydow in the movie of the same name. Eight years after the start of Farwell's mill, Thomas French, another of Fitchburg's early settlers, built the third dam across the river to run the town's first paper mill. Three years later the mill was sold to Leonard Burbank who installed a hollander, a new Dutch invention for making paper pulp from rags, that produced 100 pounds of paper a day. One of his "lay boys" was the young Alvah Crocker who later captained the Crocker Burbank Paper Company to its position as one of the world leaders of the paper industry.

At the beginning of the nineteenth century the population of Fitchburg had grown to 1390 people. The Fifth Massachusetts Turnpike, as it was called—portions of the old roadway are still called so today—passed through the town from western settlements towards Boston. Turnpike gates were often set up on privately owned land, such as that of Joseph Palmer, and a toll was exacted from the steady stream of heavily laden wagons that passed daily, carrying farm, forest, and factory products in a surge of post-war commerce. A stagecoach route, the Boston Post Road, ran through Concord, Fitchburg, Keene, and up through Windsor, Vermont on its way to Montreal. Two separate stagecoach lines, one named Marshall's and the other Twitchell's, each with over twenty coaches and 100 horses, competed for the business of carrying passengers, mail and news. Marshall's operation was headquartered in Fitchburg and Twitchell's in Worcester.

After the loss of the American colonies, England even more closely guarded her industrial secrets. They wished to keep America, whether as a colony or a separate country, a strong market for British manufactured goods. The United States remained so until well past the Civil War years. Cotton mills were set up in New England using unskilled labor and water power, but time and time again they failed.

However, the opportunity for industrial advancement came in 1789, when Samual Slater, who had learned in England how to repair machinery in a cotton mill, was able to reconstruct from memory a twenty-four spindle cotton spinning machine for a company in Pawtucket, Rhode Island. Two years later Eli Whitney invented the cotton gin. By 1820, the South, which had during the eighteenth century been hardly a competitor in the cotton market, was producing close to a million bales a year and by 1850 it was four million. This abundance of raw material, and the increased demand for use of the cotton, provided a major impetus for the beginning of the Industrial Revolution in New England.

In Fitchburg, in 1807, thirty townspeople pooled their resources and formed a stock company for the purpose of establishing a cotton mill on the Nashua River. It was the second Slater-type mill in Massachusetts and only the third such mill in the whole country. A two-story brick building was erected on the river between the Kimball mills and the scythe shop further upstream. A raceway was channeled from above the dam to under the building where it turned a large wheel that powered the spinning machines.

The Fitchburg Cotton Manufacturing Corporation was an experiment on many levels. To finance the operation the owners decreed that every man who worked for the corporation be required to own a share in the company. This kind of financial arrangement was very new to the men of Fitchburg, or anyone else for that matter, and caused no end of argument and disagreement. The only person at all familiar with this type of machine production was a Charles Robbins who had "stolen" copies of the machine patterns from Slater in Rhode Island. Robbins, apparantly a quarrelsome individual who loved his flagon of rum, demanded an equal share of the potential proceeds for doing nothing more than providing the plans for building the machines. His cohorts finally ended that problem by stealing the plans from him and then firing him from the company.

The men from Fitchburg did not know how the spinnng machine was built or how it ran before stealing Robbins' plans, and they also had no idea how to oversee or manage what was to them a large group of people working together in a single building for hours at a stretch. There were probably no more than six people in the entire country who had that kind of expertise in those days. On top of this, they encountered the problem of how to transport large quantities of ginned cotton to their various factory buildings, and how to dispatch large quantities of spun cotton out to their customers.

But these were not the worst of the company's probles. For the first two years the company prospered. A neighborhood called Factory Square, a small cluster of mill worker's houses, shops and stores grew up around the cotton mill. The company even grew and expanded to acquire the Kimball mill's dam site down river. However, the quarreling among the owners reached such a peak by 1816 that one of the directors had the dam destroyed, leaving the mill without power. This act of internecine vandalism brought about the demise of the company. The rancor among the directors of the company was so intense that they could never again cooperate with each other to get the dam rebuilt.

The first years of the nineteenth century saw an exaggerated growth of textile mills in New England, growth accelerated by President Jefferson's embargo of British goods. By 1810, there were no less than fifty-four

cotton mills in Massachusetts. In that year, a young
carpenter-turned-mechanic named Martin Newton, who
had worked on the machinery in Fitchburg's first cotton
mill, built a second cotton mill in the old Kimball fulling
mill building and set up business. He added weaving
machines, becoming one of the first companies in America
to manufacture cloth from ginned cotton in the same plant
as it was spun. Newton's mill stood as one model for
Francis Cabot Lowell, who established the Boston
Manufacturing Company in Waltham, using a newly
invented power loom. In turn, the Newton plant copied
Lowell in finding new answers to problems of material
inventory and distribution and in using young women—a
surplus of labor on New England farms—who were
willing and able to work long hours while living chastely in
dormitories near the plant. In this way the young farm
women, who quickly learned to run the water-powered
carders and spinners, worked for an average of two years.
This occupation allowed them to save for their marriage
dowry, which they could never have done on the family
farm.

Between the years of 1807 and 1815 the cotton
industry experienced a spectacular growth in the country as
a whole. Once the tariff protection against English goods
was lifted after the peace treaty of 1815, America became
flooded with less expensive cotton products, but still, the
production rate of cotton cloth rose by 15% every year
from 1815 to 1833. From then till the beginning of the
Civil War, it went up a still respectable 5% every year.
Cotton textiles led the American manufacturing boom
prior to the Civil War, one of the major reasons being the
ratio of transportation weight of cotton to its selling price.
Raw cotton and finished cloth, unlike products made of

iron or wood, is so much lighter in bulk that it could be transported to cotton mills located anyplace that had an adequate supply of water power.

Right behind the manufacturing growth of cotton cloth in the United States was that of woolen cloth. The first of the woolen mills in Fitchburg was established in the old cotton mill in Factory Square. With use of the newly invented spinning jenny and Goulding condenser that compacted the wool, one person could produce over 700 skeins of wool a day as opposed to the hand spinning wheel on which a housewife could turn out four skeins a day. Merino sheep were introduced into New England from Spain in 1810 and by the 1830s there were over 28,000 sheep in Worcester County. Even with the homegrown supply of raw material, though, wool could not compete with cotton because animal fiber is much harder to control with machines and wool cloth is more difficult to clean.

Overall production rates for all industries in the United States, prior to the Civil War, rose at an average rate of 6.7% every year. The Fitchburg plants almost exactly mirrored the country's increase in manufactured goods. However, roughly one third of this growth rate can be attributed to an increase in raw materials and transportation, and advances and refinements in technology. Another third can be laid to an increase in demand from a growing population and a resultant drop in prices. The last third is attributed to a learn-by-doing curve on the part of mill employees. Both managers and workers got better at the factory system as time went by. Workers learned to be more efficient at running and feeding the machines. Managers improved in their efforts to extract a higher piece-per-hour rate from their labor force. Since factory work was not skilled labor, anyone could do it. It was monotonous and unhealthy, but it was not necessarily dangerous and did not require close concentration. Even a child could work twelve to fourteen hour days, and many did. In the 1820s it was estimated that 45% of all workers in textile mills in New England were children. Another 30% were women and of the remaining 25%, the men, many were employed as foremen, managers, or in machine maintenance.

THE COMING OF THE RAILROAD

In 1834, the town of Fitchburg had 400 private home two paper mills, four gristmills, eleven saw mills, two woolen mills, and four cotton mills. They also manufactured scythes, hats, buggy whips, chairs, and window blinds. Stagecoach lines connected Fitchburg to Boston, New York, and Montreal. Throughout the 1830s, the town's economy, like the rest of New England, expanded at an over-inflated rate until it crashed in the Panic of 1837. The population of Massachusetts in general, which had been second in numbers in the nation at the end of the Revolutionary War, was now eighth, behind other port states such as New York and Pennsylvania, and behind even some frontier states like Ohio and Tennessee. Sales of farm crops in New England were down due to depletion of nutrients in the soil which had been tilled for four generations. Farmers and shopkeepers began putting their money into new ventures in manufacturing whose growth had now leveled off after the Wall Street panic.

Transportation became the critical issue for industrial growth. The woolen mills in Worcester County could process four times the amount of wool grown by local sheep farms. Like wool, cotton cloth production was limited by the amount of raw material that could be shipped by wagon over the turnpike from Boston. The 100,000 cords of firewood, needed to heat the houses in Boston each winter, were brought by boat from Maine instead of the shorter distance from places like Fitchburg because of the difficulty in transporting it over dirt roads.

The city of Worcester, to the south, had completed a canal to Rhode Island in 1828, which helped buoy its economy, and because of this new mode of transportation, the city shifted its commercial focus toward New York and away from Boston. The great port of Boston began to lag behind New York and Philadelphia simply because of the difficulty in moving imported material and exported goods to and from the western part of the state and into New York State. To solve the problem, the Boston, Worcester and Albany Railroad Line was begun.

In Fitchburg, a group of industrialists, led by Alvah Crocker, drummed up local support for the Fitchburg Railroad, which was completed in 1845. Crocker himself negotiated with each landowner along the route of the proposed tracks for the price of the right-of-way across their land. He traveled to England to purchase the rails needed for the track. In Boston, he recruited, as track layers, newly-arrived Irishmen who had come to escape the Potato Famine that was ravaging their country. The immigrants established a foothold in their new home with the men laying the track, and the women and children finding employment in the Fitchburg mills during the boom which resulted from the opening of the railroad line.

With the coming of the railroad, Fitchburg experienced a sustained industrial and economic growth for many decades to come, through the Civil War years and up into the next century. In 1845 the town had 3,883 people, the following year over 5,000. Within the next two years the rail line had extended to Brattleboro, Vermont in the north and Worcester to the south. A local doctor at the time described Fitchburg as "like a seaport crowded with teams, carriages of every description and full of people."

AN INDUSTRIAL CENTER

Ushered in with the railroad was the growth of the iron foundries and building of steam engines. Fitchburg's iron and machine industry dated back to the time under British rule when small shops on the streams that fed the Nashua River made tools and guns, which was illegal under English law. Farwell's scythe shop, begun in the decade after the Revolutionary War, grew to become, by 1847, the oldest scythe manufacturer in New England, furnishing more scythes than any town in the country. John Farwell had married Hannah Thurston, sister to Asa and Cyrus Thurston and aunt of Frances Thurston who married Henry J. Lowe. Abel Simonds, who married into the Farwell family, took over the business in 1851 and by the next year Fitchburg was turning out over 84,000 finished scythes a year. When the invention of McCormick's reaper pulled the bottom out of the scythe market, Simonds switched to making saws and became one of the largest saw makers in the country. Simonds Manufacturing Company, which later became Simonds Saw and Steel Company, was a model of both financial and manufacturing management. In 1921, Abel Simonds' grandson, Gifford Simonds, left his position as treasurer and brought his financial expertise with him when he took over the directorship of the Waltham Watch Company.

Fitchburg's industry was originally founded on water power. In 1837 there were eleven dams on the Nashua River, within the town limits, and sites for several more which were not yet built. By the end of the nineteenth century there were between thirty and forty dams being utilized in the same stretch of water. With its new role as a New England railroad hub, the town was in a position to take advantage of the country's growing need for machinery. Another successful Fitchburg scythe company, owned by Augustus Whitman and Eugene Miles, shifted its production to the manufacture of pick axes, mowing machines and reaper knives, and Bowie knives used during the Civil War.

John and Salmon Putnam, two young machinists, set up shop to repair and build textile and paper machine tools in 1838. In 1849, with Charles H. Brown, who had previously built steam engines for Otis Tufts in Boston, they began to manufacture stationary steam engines and other machine tools. They were joined the next year by Charles R. Burleigh, who also came from Otis Tufts' shop. The Putnam Machine Company was incorporated in 1858, selling stationary steam engines throughout the country. Charles H. Brown left the next year and set up C.H Brown and Company. Charles Burleigh later invented the Burleigh drill and air compressor which was used to complete the Hoosac Tunnel for the rail line to New York state. The Burleigh drill was later sold all over the world.

For a time, Fitchburg was known as the "Machine City" supplying the country with steam engines and machine tools. Near the new train depot a foundry was opened that could pour an iron casting weighing five hundred pounds, a feat considered so stupendous by the citizens of the city that a large crowd gathered to see its first operation. The C. H. Brown company manufactured a newly-invented automatic cut-off steam engine that was later used by Thomas Edison in his experiments in Menlo Park. Brown's automatic steam engine was also installed in the Elgin National Watch Company in Elgin, Illinois to run their entire expanded plant. With the addition of several other companies before the end of the Civil War, Fitchburg became a leader in the steam engine and machine tool industry.

Several smaller, but no less important, industries grew during the pre-war period as a result of the railroad. The Heywood Furniture Company made chairs with machines manufactured in the same town. Sylvanus Sawyer located his rattan-cutting factory in Fitchburg to be near the railroad that brought in the supply of raw material, and also so he could supply Heywood's chair factory with rattan for the seats. Sawyer also began manufacturing rifled cannons during the war, and the Nashua River ran a deep blue from dyes used at Factory Square for making Union uniforms. Due to the boycott of cotton from the South, that industry slowed for the early years of the war and then picked up again with cotton imports from Egypt and the Far East.

ECONOMIC GROWTH

The year 1857 saw a new nation-wide financial panic brought about by over-speculation in railroads by such people as Jay Gould and Cornelius Vanderbilt. Over 5,000 factories, banks, stock companies and railroads went bankrupt in that year. Fitchburg, however, felt only minor shock waves of the panic. A few companies went under but the banks in the town remained sound, due to their policy of loaning only small amounts of money and then only to local businesses. Alvah Crocker's railroad, actually the town's railroad, remained on solid ground, turning a profit as it had done since its inauguration.

The War of Southern Rebellion may have bankrupted the Union government, but the economy of industrial towns like Fitchburg held fairly steady. Except for the woolen industry whose product rate soared with the manufacture of uniforms, the other industries in the town—cotton, paper, machinery—leveled off or dropped slightly in some cases. Prices for commodities inflated during the war, bringing in a higher price for individual items. Unfortunately for the workers, wages tend to lag behind prices, so that inflationary prices were realized only as profits by the owners.

The Fitchburg Fusilers, which included two Massachusetts regiments, depleted the ranks of factory workers when they marched south to see action in places like Antietam, Port Hudson, Louisiana, Gettysburg and the Wilderness. Back home, new workers came to fill their spots and the population of the town actually grew during the war years. Fitchburg donated nearly $125,000—a hefty sum in those days—to the war effort. New buildings continued to be built and new companies started. Sylvester C. Wright left the Putnam Machine Company in 1863 to begin what later became Fitchburg Machine Company, using his own newly designed machine patterns to make lathes, shapers, and machinists' tools that were shipped to England and also sold to the Union Pacific Railroad. Wright's company moved into a new building on lower

Main Street in 1865, built by his friend, Sylvanus Sawyer.

There are some economic historians who argue that the Civil War was a watershed, or dividing line, in America's economy. Before the war, we were an agrarian-driven economy and after the war an industry-driven one. Others argue that the war was no more than an interruption in a steady growth of both areas. From 1840 to 1860, the rate of American-made manufactured goods rose by an average 7.6% per year; after the war, the growth rate from 1865 to 1891 was 6.6% per year. The commodity growth rate of all American products, including agricultural products, before the war was 4.6% per year, and after the war was 4.4% per year. Whichever way one views the country's transformation from an agrarian to an industrial culture, the Commonwealth of Massachusetts helped lead the way, and Fitchburg was in the vanguard of that transformation. Beginning as a farming community, its industry outdistanced its agricultural interests by the time of the Civil War to the extent that, of the few farms left in the community, all were dedicated to raising food for those who worked in the town's industries.

Industrial growth in Fitchburg continued after the war. With the resumption of cotton shipments from the South and a new demand for machine products, the town's industrial growth rate quickly equaled that of the pre-war years. There were many new start-up manufacturers like the Haskins Machine Company, which was soon winning prizes at the Luxemburg International Exhibition of Machinery.

POPULATION GROWTH

By 1871 the town had reached a population of over 10,000 people and in 1872 they incorporated themselves as a city. They elected their first mayor, and floated a bond for $500,000 to build a water reservoir. They levied an income tax for those who earned over $5,000 a year. This was a great deal of money at a time when the average factory worker earned no more than $500 a year, but in Fitchburg there were enough of these people who earned over $5,000 a year to make a substantial difference in contributions to the city's coffers. In addition to the income tax there was a "Betterment Tax" on those homes that were bettered by new public services such as water and sewer lines. If political differences were strong when Fitchburg was a town, the battles became fierce once they were officially a city. Every single industrialist in the newly-formed city took the city to court, suing for abatement of the water tax imposed on their company. Many felt there was no need to spend money for sewage lines, that the sewage could continue to drain into the Nashua River the way it had always done. And, of course, since only the most wealthy citizens were affected by the new income tax, it was hotly contested in the courts as well as in city hall.

The 1860s and early 1870s saw a new influx of immigration. Impoverished French-Canadian farmers came south to work in the factories of Fitchburg and Lowell in Massachusetts or Manchester and Nashua in New Hampshire. New arrivals from Europe, landing in Boston, traveled west, but those that soon ran out of money stopped to find jobs in the factories in central Massachusetts. By the time Fitchburg became a city, over twenty percent of its population were foreign born. New arrivals found work in the cotton and woolen mills, the paper companies, or the boiler and machine factories. They found housing in "The Patch," an area of small lots deeded originally by Alvah Crocker to Irish railroad workers, in the old shanties abandoned by an earlier generation who had "moved up."

THE RIVER

It was mostly due to conditions in "The Patch," originally built on land that Sylvanus Sawyer still owned, that the political battle for the installation of sewers in the city was won by the proponents of the new sewage system in 1872. The death rate from typhoid, cholera, diphtheria, tetanus, tuberculosis, and scarlet fever was five times higher in the lower end of the city than it was in the upper sections. Local physicians lobbied heavily for an end to dumping domestic and industrial sewage into the Nashua River. The river, long the city's lifeline had also become its death angel. Sawyer, elected as alderman from the sixth ward, the area at the lower end of Main Street, worked extensively for the clean-up of the river, complaining that the river's stench alone could kill a person.

The ongoing battle of the river, which goes back to arguments between the first and the second mill owners in the very early years of the nineteenth century, continues even up to the present day. In 1876, a study by the state Board of Health found that Fitchburg, along with the town of Clinton down river, were the worst polluters of a river in the entire state. Laws were passed against industrial river pollution in the 1890s, but were difficult to enforce. Finally, in the 1970s, with funding from the federal government, the Nashua River Watershed Association began the latest and biggest campaign to clean up the river. Two water treatment plants have been built in Fitchburg, one at the upper end, at the mouth of the Nashua, and another just before the river leaves the city limits to flow into Leominster. Strong legislation has been passed to control polluting by the mills and factories that still remain on the river.

THE FITCHBURG BOARD OF TRADE

The Wall Street Panic of September, 1873 ushered in the worst economic depression the country had known until that time. The depression was to last until 1878. Fitchburg was hit hard by the economic downturn. Over-speculation and over-expansion in manufacturing and in the railroads left companies, banks and stockholders with worthless shares and loans. Steam engine, machine and tool orders dropped off precipitously as new ventures and some not-so-new ventures went under. Prices for paper and cotton and wool cloth dropped to a pre-war level. Layoffs from the mills left many workers destitute and many owners were pushed over the line into bankruptcy.

After the first hard winter, in the spring of 1874, several factory owners, bankers, and tradesmen formed the Fitchburg Board of Trade. The roster of founding members read like the city's Who's Who—Crocker, Simonds, Wallace, Miles, Sawyer, Palmer, Lowe, Putnam, Haskins, Fosdick, Brown, Wright. The purpose of the board was to stimulate the business climate of the city. Local newspapers called the group the "Fitchburg Hustlers" for their dynamic enthusiasm to do for their community what had become nearly impossible for the rest of the country—to pull the city up by its own economic bootstraps. Industry had pulled them through down times in the 1830s and the 1850s and, by God, it could do it again. They shored up existing companies experiencing hard times, and they brought in experts from other parts of the country to consult with them on how to find better markets for their goods or better ways of transporting those goods. With the accumulated years of experience and hard-headed knowledge among members of the board, they felt certain they could make a success of anything on which they set their focus.

The board's first task was to take on the debt of the Worcester North Agricultural Society. This union of producers in northern Worcester county was the organization central to providing the city with its almost entire food intake. The board issued one hundred and twenty $100 bonds bearing a 3% interest rate which would be paid in five years, and they financed mortgages for farmland by issuing $50 bonds payable in five years.

Two of the board's more courageous ventures were their entrepreneurial efforts put forth on behalf of setting up new companies that might broaden the base for job opportunities, while at the same time, increasing the city's prestige as an innovative industrial center. The first of these ventures was the watch company, and second, six months later, was a fast-loom company for making suspender webbing. The fast-loom company used a new patent recently awarded to a Fitchburg native, and the watch company used a variation on a watch movement design previously rendered for high quality timepieces.

The Board of Trade did help the city through the depression, and then continued once the city and the country as a whole saw more prosperous times. Several companies that would otherwise have gone under during the depression were kept afloat, and jobs were maintained or created to keep people working. Fifty years later, in the early 1920s, the Board of Trade became the Fitchburg Chamber of Commerce. With the waning of America's, and thus the city's, Industrial Age in the 1970s, the Chamber of Commerce saw its effectiveness ebbing. In 1990, they elected to become a part of the North Central Massachusetts Chamber of Commerce, where the spirit of 1874 is still alive and working to bring renewed spark to the area.

Expanding the Crocker Burbank textile mills as part of Fitchburg's rapid growth in the nineteenth century..

Photo courtesy of the Fitchburg Historical Society

Sylvanus Sawyer 1822 - 1895

Chapter 6

MEN OF THEIR TIME

Of the many people on the Fitchburg Board of Trade who were connected with the beginning of the watch company, two men may be credited with the actual launching of the enterprise. Sylvanus Sawyer and Henry J. Lowe directed the organizing of the company. Sawyer invested his own money and made the broader decisions such as how the venture should be capitalized, where the factory would be housed, and who would be hired to do the work. Lowe provided the expertise necessary for the design of the watch to be made and what machinery would be needed to make it.

Upon the recommendations of a special committee headed by Thomas Palmer, the Board of Trade made the decision to organize a watch company in Fitchburg. The first step was to appoint a director, the obvious choice being Sylvanus Sawyer, one of their own members. As experienced as any of the board members in the entrepreneurial art of starting a manufacturing firm, Sawyer had an added advantage of knowing something about the financial pitfalls inherent in the watch business— and, in fact, already owned certain watchmaking tooling and machinery. Sawyer had been a major stockholder in the United States Watch Company in Marion, New Jersey. When that company failed in 1875, Sawyer lost a substantial amount of money. To recoup a portion of this loss he took possession of some of the machinery the U.S. Watch Company had developed, with the hopes of using it to manufacture what would be their best line, 17-size, ¼-plate and bridge model.

In all probability, when the Fitchburg Board of Trade was casting about for ideas on what kind of new manufacturing business to start in their city, it must have been Sylvanus Sawyer who promoted the idea of a watch company. It was so like Sawyer's character to plant a seed and then watch it grow, something he had been doing, both literally and figuratively, all his life. Since the 1840s, he had started several companies and invested seed money in several others. He was also, from his early childhood, fascinated with the growth and hybridization of domestic and exotic flowers.

It was Sawyer's idea to hire Lowe as superintendent of the fledgling company. Lowe was the perfect man for the job. Not only was he a member of one of Fitchburg's founding families, he was an expert watchmaker. He had worked for the U.S. Watch Company in New Jersey for seven years prior to their bankruptcy, the last five of those years he functioned as one of three superintendents of the firm. As such, he had intimate knowledge of the ¼-plate and bridge movement, designed under his leadership, as well as the machinery used to produce it. Prior to his employment at the United States Watch Company, Lowe had his own watchmaker's shop on upper Main Street in Fitchburg for over twenty years.

A LIFELONG FRIENDSHIP

It is not difficult to imagine that Sawyer and Lowe were close friends. They certainly knew each other well, belonging, for most of their adult lives, to the same social set. Even though they were different in many ways, there was much they had in common. Probably the most significant thing they shared was an ancestor. Sylvanus Sawyer's great grandfather was Henry J. Lowe's great, great grandfather. Besides this, both Sylvanus and Henry were born in 1822 on farms, about fifteen miles apart, Sawyer in Templeton and Lowe in Fitchburg. They were both sickly and frail as children, leaving them unable to perform the heavy farm chores carried out by their respective brothers. Relieved of farm duties, Sawyer and Lowe each found a way to indulge his curiosity in the workings of different kinds of machinery. Sawyer's fascination lay with larger types of mechanization like sawmills or steam-driven engines. Lowe's attention found itself riveted by the smallest of machines, the pocket watch.

This difference of focus characterized their personalities for the rest of their lives. Sawyer's perspective was always broad, designing a tool or solving one kind of problem and then moving on to the next thing that captured his interest. Lowe focused his attention on the workings of the pocket watch at an early age and never left it. These same traits carried over to Lowe's and Sawyer's personal lives as well. Lowe married at the age of twenty-three, had nine children and died in the arms of his loving wife at the age of fifty-four. Sawyer never married, but moved always in the elite circles of Fitchburg's political and social life until his death at the age of seventy-three. He was described in newspaper articles as always being in demand at dinner parties and social gatherings due to his affable demeanor and his fine manners.

Both of these men personified America's industrial century. The span of their lives encompassed the transition from an almost totally agrarian economy in the early part of the century to a predominantly industrial one in the later part. Sawyer was born in Templeton, Massachusetts, a small farming community to the west of Fitchburg. He died in 1895 at his mansion on Summer Street in Fitchburg, only six years after the inauguration of William Henry Harrison who won his election on the issue of the Gold Standard that marked the beginning of America's industrial economy. Lowe was born in Fitchburg when the town was still a farming community. He died in 1876 at his home on the corner of Blossom and Green Street in Fitchburg, just when the city was coming into its own as an industrial center.

THE SAWYER FAMILY

Sylvanus Sawyer's father, Balcom Sawyer, known in the community as Praying John, owned a comfortable-sized farm and, like his British forebears, operated a commercial sawmill for the local community. The Sawyers claimed an ancestry dating back to the Saxon mercenary soldiers who accompanied the Norman knights brought over to England by William the Conqueror in 1066. Thomas Sawyer emigrated to America in the 1640s and settled in the Massachusetts Bay Colony in Charlestown. In 1650, he struck out for the wilderness and settled in Lancaster, Massachusetts near where the two branches of the Nashua River come together. His son, Thomas Jr., later sold the sawmill he had helped his father build and moved further west to the town of Sterling, Massachusetts. In 1705, he and his son Elias, like John Fitch several years later, was captured by Indians and force-marched to Quebec. There he found favor with the French governor and was able to obtain freedom for himself and his son by advancing French sawmill technology, adding many improvements of his own and other Yankee mill owners.

One of Thomas's grandsons, John, later moved to Templeton to farm. This was Sylvanus's grandfather. John's brother, Phineas, moved to Fitchburg to farm. This was Henry J. Lowe's great grandfather. The two men, Sylvanus and Henry, would have been, according to genealogical terminology, what is known as second cousins, once removed.

THE LOWE FAMILY

Henry J. Lowe's great grandfather, Joseph Lowe, moved to Fitchburg from Ipswich, Massachusetts in 1763 to carve a farm out of the wilderness. He married Mary Sawyer, daughter of Phineas and grandmother of Henry. By the time Henry was married to Frances Thurston in 1845, he was related by blood, or by marriage, to half the town. Several of his brothers and sisters, as well as his aunts, uncles and cousins married people from other prominent Fitchburg families with names like Farwell, Putnam, Kimball, Whitney, Merriam, Torrey, Wallace and Thurston—Henry also had an uncle married to a Thurston. Throughout the nineteenth century, the name Lowe could be found on the roster of just about every stock company, board, or council in the city. They served the community as businessmen, entrepreneurs, industrialists, bankers, city councilmen, and two mayors. Joseph Lowe, Henry's cousin, died fighting for the Union in 1863 in "Bloody Kansas" in a raid by Quantrell's guerrillas. A nephew, Arthur H. Lowe, upon election to seat of president of the Fitchburg Board of Trade in 1891, rejuvenated what had become a languishing organization. One cousin married Thomas Palmer's daughter, Emma, and their son, Erving Lowe, became, like his grandfather, an eminent Fitchburg dentist. It would be a gross understatement to say that Henry J. Lowe was a son of the city of Fitchburg. Merely by virtue of who he was, aside from the fact that he had achieved a high mechanical skill as a watchmaker, he was the very soul of the city itself.

THE BUDDING INVENTOR

Balcom Sawyer, John's son, had three sons— Joseph, Sylvanus, and Addison. The oldest and youngest boys joined their father in the working of the farm and mill. Sylvanus spent his childhood in the mill's machine shop, making and repairing tools and mill parts, tinkering, and experimenting with new ways of transferring power from the mill wheel to the sawblade. To accomplish these tasks, his father acquired for him a mandril, an early hand-driven lathe.

One section of the Sawyer farm acres was set aside for apple and pear orchards. Here Sylvanus' father taught him how to graft fruit trees and the two experimented with several kinds of hardier and more abundant crops. Between the machine shop and the orchard, the young Sylvanus spent what was, for him, an idyllic childhood. He was able to both distract himself from his physical ill health and provide himself with two pursuits that became his lifelong passions: developing innovations to machine tools, and hybridizing plants to produce hardier versions. His talent lay in his ability to take apart a mechanism and understand the principle of what made it work. At the age of fourteen, he took apart a clock—more than likely it was a punched brass plate of the type made in Connecticut—that his father had relegated to the basement because he could not get it to work. Sylvanus found the source of the trouble, repaired it, then cleaned and oiled the clock, which kept relatively good time for years afterward. Old Balcom, proud of this achievement, no doubt bragged about his son's God-given talent to the members of the Congregational Church on Sunday, which was probably why Sylvanus found himself repairing any number of stubbornly ill-tempered clocks and pocket watches for people in the village.

For his sixteenth birthday his parents gave him a musical instrument called a harmonica. This little mouth organ, introduced to America only a few years before, had been invented in Germany, around the time of Sylvanus's birth, by a man named Friedrich Buschmann who patterned it after an ancient Chinese musical instrument similar to a harmonica, called a *sheng*. Sylvanus's joy in

119

playing the harmonica soon took second place to his need to take the thing apart to see how it worked. The free-floating reed that made a different note whether the air was blown in or sucked out fascinated the young man, who immediately set about trying to build a keyboard instrument on the same principle, using a bellows for the air supply.

It took him almost a year to complete the kind of instrument that would be called, in later years, a *reed organ* or *harmonium*. The bellows, operated by a person other than the musician, blew air in or sucked it out and the pressing of a key determined which reed would be affected by the air. This latest achievement might also have became the subject of Balcom's crowing at church, and it is not unlikely the new instrument was played in concert with a fiddle on Saturday nights to entertain the family and their friends from the surrounding farms. And it no doubt accompanied the hymns of the Sunday morning services in the town's clapboard Congregational Church. News of this new reed organ would have reached the ears of the district's itinerant music teacher, a man by the name of Cyrus Thurston, brother to the Hawaiian missionary, Asa Thurston. Cyrus made periodic rounds to small villages within a fifteen-mile radius of Fitchburg to teach music in churches, one-room schoolhouses and farmhouse parlors. But Sylvanus' reed organ was never really developed. A similar instrument, invented in 1818 in Vienna by a man named Anton Haeckl, and later introduced to the American colonies, had the added advantage of a foot treadle that could be pumped by the person playing the keyboard.

By contrast, not that much is known about Henry Lowe's childhood. By the time he was seventeen, in

1839, the family had moved to a large house on Mechanic Street near Fitchburg's upper common. His father and two of the younger brothers had established a business, buying and selling livestock, their own and that of other farmers in the area. In the fall of that year, Henry became apprenticed to a watchmaker, S.H. Goodnow, at his shop in the Torrey and Wood block of Main Street just a few blocks away from the Lowe home.

In early winter of 1839, when the apple harvest was done, Balcom Sawyer made arrangements with his son-in-law in Augusta, Maine for Sylvanus to apprentice with him in the gunsmith trade. Sylvanus balked at his father's decision, asking why could he not just as easily apprentice to a gunsmith or watchmaker in Fitchburg. But his argument did not prevail and he was sent off to Maine where the rough conditions of life and the coldness of the Maine winter conspired to bring his health to an all-time low. Within three months of being sent to his brother-in-law's house, Sylvanus was back home in Templeton.

After a few bed-ridden weeks at home under his mother's care, he found himself back in the farm's machine shop and forge, putting to use what he had so quickly learned in Maine. He fashioned a new rifle for his father and, with his brothers helping him, began taking orders for guns from neighbors. In the late winter months of 1840, before spring planting, he and his brothers built a wood-burning steam engine under Sylvanus's direction, probably inspired by Robert Fulton's steamboats which had by that time become ubiquitous on America's rivers. The Sawyer engine had a four way valve and type of screw propeller mounted on a flat-bottomed boat. In the spring runoff, they navigated the little steamboat up the Otter River to Winchendon and then into the Millers River to Royalston.

Not satisfied with just water trafficking, Sylvanus's next project was a small foot-pedal powered car—he called it a "hand-car"— on the order of a bicycle, but with four wheels instead of two, and the brothers could often be seen pedaling this strange vehicle on the muddy roads to town. Between projects and repairing neighbors' clocks and watches, and fashioning firearms, Sylvanus also found time to turn gentlemen's canes and umbrellas on his mandrel, carving interesting and intricate designs into the wood, and then selling them to the same neighbors whose timepieces he repaired. That same summer he began experimenting with growing strains of domestic strawberries and grapes inside a cold-frame hothouse he built on the side of the sawmill building.

1840s COMING OF AGE

In the fall of 1844, when the apples were in, Sylvans took the stagecoach into Boston. His reputation as an inventive machinist preceded him and he was hired by the Jones and Hobbs Company, makers of locks and house trimmings, to improve their manufacturing process. In Boston, Sylvanus reveled in the hustle and bustle of the growing port city and, with great enthusiasm, threw himself into his work.

Henry Lowe, meanwhile, had served an apprenticeship of five years, giving him the necessary knowledge to go into business for himself. His family advanced him money to open his own shop on the corner of Main and Central Streets where he provided, for the next twenty-three years, service in watch cleaning and repair to what would have been either Swiss going barrel, bar movements or English fusee, full-plate movements. Once established in his own business, Henry was finally able to obtain the necessary permission from Cyrus Thurston to marry his daughter, Frances. In January of 1845, Henry and Frances Thurston were married at the Rollstone Congregational Church. Henry's father died of tuberculosis that year, and his mother succumbed to the same disease four years later.

The year 1846 saw Sylvanus Sawyer on the road to making his first great fortune. He left Boston and was brought to Phillipston, Massachusetts, the next town west of Templeton, to make adjustments to the machinery of a caning factory run by a William Wood. He would have been able to ride the new railroad line that had been just recently completed from Boston to Fitchburg and then take the stage line to Phillipston. The position proved not challenging enough for Sylvanus and, later that same year, he was back in Boston, working for Otis Tufts to learn what he could about steam engines. At Otis Tufts's machine shop in East Boston, he worked with men who he would meet again in Fitchburg and know for the rest of his life, men such as Charles H. Brown, Charles R. Burleigh, and Louis DeBlais Bartlett.

A tremendous demand for cut strips of rattan existed in the 1840s. Raw material was plentiful and cheap, as well as lightweight and easy to transport by ship. Caned chair seats were very much in fashion, being more comfortable than shaped wooden seats. In the 1850s, hoops of rattan competed with extruded wire to be used in ladies' skirts to hold the round shape of their hem. Cutting the lengths of rattan into strips, though, was a long and expensive project due to the fact that the knife blades for cutting were dulled so quickly by the coating, or enamel, on the outside of the rattan.

Sawyer worked for Otis Tufts until 1848 when his brother Joseph brought him out to Palmer, Massachusetts to improve production in Wakefield's rattan mill where Joseph was employed. In 1846, while still at Otis Tufts, Sylvanus was given a patent for a machine that scraped and gauged rattan. At Palmer, he devised a new way of cutting the rattan strips based on the principle of running the knife up inside the cane, separating the strands and cutting so as not to touch the blade-dulling enamel. He left Palmer after a year and returned to Templeton to develop the knife and start his own company. In 1849 he was given a patent for his new knife called a Tubular Spurred Cutter, and later called a Star Knife. His new idea has dominated the cutting of rattan from 1850 to the present day.

With the coming of the railroad, the town of Fitchburg erupted with new commerce. Imported goods and raw materials transported on ocean going vessels were carried by rail from the port of Boston inland at a speed that was astounding to people accustomed to moving at the pace of horse, or ox-drawn, wagons. Factories and mills in a wide radius around Fitchburg could now ship their products with speed and an ease undreamed of before. People who never traveled further than a few miles from home now came to Fitchburg to board passenger cars to depots like Concord or Waltham.

Henry Lowe's business thrived during this time. He could probably have been a success in Fitchburg merely by handling those watches belonging to his extended family there, but the increase in commercial dealers, shipping agents and manufacturers in the town magnified his watch business to a degree that he could barely keep up with the demand for his services. Also, more people in the area were buying watches. A small, mill owner who might previously have needed to tell the time no more accurately than by the rising and the setting of the sun, now needed to know what time the train arrived each day or whether his employees arrived to the factory on time. Lowe, like most other individual watchmakers, was also expanding the line of watches he imported for resale.

Henry's brothers began shipping their livestock, pigs, cows, and sheep into Boston by rail. The ready market they found for their meat products gave them the opportunity to greatly increase their livestock brokerage. Soon they were making more money buying and selling than by raising their own. Over the next thirty years the Lowe Brothers Livestock Company grew prosperous providing beef and pork to the city of Boston.

In June of 1847 Henry and Frances had their first child, a girl they named Helen Frances. Two years later, in October of 1849, her sister, Louise, was born. They made their home on Mechanic Street near both the Lowe and the Thurston family homesteads.

1850s BIG BUSINESS

At the same time that Sylvanus was working on perfecting his rattan knife, his father's brother, also named Joseph Sawyer, of Royalston, Massachusetts, along with Walter Heywood, in Fitchburg, was working on the same idea. There was a race on between the uncle and his nephews as to who would be the first to be awarded the patent. Sylvanus, with the help of his brother, Joseph, won the race. Uncle Joseph and Walter Heywood then merged their business into the nephews' enterprise and helped create The American Rattan Company, a small rattan cutting plant, centered in Templeton. At the same time, Heywood's family created the Heywood Furniture Company that helped to make the city of Gardner into what later came to be known as the chair capital of the world. Uncle Joseph continued working on his rattan knife design and applied for another patent in 1854, but his new invention failed to meet the purpose of the design.

Using Sylvanus's newly invented rattan knife the American Rattan Company could produce rattan strips at twice the volume and half the price of its closest competitor. The business grew and flourished. In 1851 another patent was awarded to Sylvanus and his brother Addison for a machine that removed rattan joints. Demand surpassed supply. Soon they were unable to bring in raw material fast enough to keep up with production schedules. So, in 1852, they formed a stock company and moved the operation to Fitchburg, setting up in a factory located a block from the railway depot.

Over the next few years, the American Rattan Compny became one of the leading manufacturers of rattan strips in the world. The Fitchburg Railroad carried daily carloads of unstripped cane from the Boston seaport and carloads of cut rattan back to Boston to be loaded on ships for foreign markets. As railway lines were laid south to Worcester and New York, west to Albany and the western states, and north to Vermont and Montreal, they carried Sawyer's rattan. Heywood Furniture in Fitchburg became one of the largest chair manufacturers in the northeast, and used enormous quantities of American Rattan Company's product.

The Sawyer brothers became very wealthy. Sylvanus, though, was not one for running a day-to-day business. His concern was, as always, how to make his machines better, more efficient. He devised a new feeding apparatus for the uncut cane and helped Addison devise a new tubular spurred cutter for which Addison was awarded the patent. But by 1854, Sylvanus had left the management of the company and set himself up to work on an idea that preoccupied since he learned of the new rifled field gun designed in Europe. In 1855, Sylvanus was given a patent for his new rifled cannon, the patent registered in America, England and France.

By 1857 Sawyer had become one of Fitchburg's leading citizens. From the time he first moved to Fitchburg, he had been a member of the congregation of the Rollstone Congregational Church on Main Street and, with his affable manner, was a desired guest at dinners and balls in Fitchburg society. This same social set also included his cousin Henry J. Lowe and Henry's wife, Frances.

Things went well for Henry and Frances through the 1850s. In 1851, Henry sold his watch business to two gentlemen named Kimball and Whitcomb. Eight months later, he bought it back. In January of 1857 their third child was born, another girl who they named Jennie Maria. The following January their first son, Charles, arrived. Henry's health remained delicate, though. He suffered from a chronic stomach ailment that had periodically flared and subsided since childhood. On days that he was too sick to work, to keep the business flourishing, he hired a young man named William Learned from Montague, Massachusetts about twenty five miles to the west of Fitchburg. William had also been apprenticed to S.H. Goodnow and had worked for Goodnow until his business was taken over by an enterprising Irishman named Reuben Conn in 1855. Possessed of a somewhat feisty personality, William Learned was nonetheless a skilled watchmaker who had a flare for business organization. Learned, however, did not last long, but went to work for the burgeoning watch manufacturing company in Waltham.

Not long after moving to Fitchburg in 1852, Sylvanus Sawyer bought a five-acre plot of land at the lower end of Main Street. The land bordered the Nashua River where the river made a wide bend before heading due south. Here on this flat, fertile piece of land he put in his gardens and built his greenhouses so he could pursue his other great passion, experimenting with hybrid flowers and fruits. He planted pear and plum trees outside and domestic strawberries and different types of grapes inside the greenhouses. At the edge of the property, on Summer Street, he built two mansions, one for himself and another for a spinster sister.

On the river side of the property there already existed a shanty town, The Patch, inhabited by the Irish immigrants who settled there in the 1840s. Even though "The Patch" was an eyesore and a reputed spreader of disease, Sylvanus saw no reason to evict its inhabitants. Rather, he did what he could to help the people in The Patch, showing them how to get a better yield in the garden patches sowed behind their shacks, and helping some find employment in his companies.

Shortly after buying property at the lower end of Main Street, down-river from the mills that had sprung up along its banks, Sylvanus began a campaign that would involve him for the rest of his life, that of trying to force the town and later the city of Fitchburg to clean up the river. He did not know at the time—no one knew—that it was the river itself, much more than the shanty town, which fostered and spread the cholera, tetanus, and typhus, diseases that took the lives of so many at the lower end of Main Street. Sylvanus's original campaign was focused mainly on trying to eliminate the horrible stench that came off the river.

Throughout 1854 and the winter of 1855, Sylvanus worked on his design for a rifled cannon. A few years prior to this, in 1851, at the Crystal Palace Exhibition in London, a German armorer named Alfred Krupp displayed a new type of field gun whose barrel, instead of being made with the usual bronze, was made of cast steel with rifling inside. Krupp was selling guns all over Europe and the Middle East. As soon as Sylvanus suceeded in getting the rattan company set up and running well without him, he began working on his own ideas for a similarly rifled cannon. Just as he had taken the principle of the small harmonica—the mouth organ—and applied it to a larger instrument, the reed organ, here he took the principle of the new smaller-bored rifled musket and applied it to an 80 millimeter cannon. His rifled cannon, which involved laminating the inside bore of the cannon with an alloyed metal that contained the rifling grooves, had the obvious advantage over the smooth bore of increased accuracy over longer distance.

The Sawyer gun first saw action in the Crimean War in 1855. The British army bought an entire battery of the new rifled cannons for use in the year-long siege of Sevastopol. Sylvanus also presented his designs to the United States Secretary of War, and in 1856, a General Ellsworth, accompanied by General Ambrose Burnside, came to Fitchburg to inspect the rifled cannon for the Department of Ordinance. Burnside, at this time, was managing a plant in Bristol, Rhode Island, making pistols. He had resigned his West Point commission several years earlier, but when the Civil War broke out, he was made a

Major General, serving under McClellan, Hooker and Grant. He himself served, for a short time, as commander of all the federal forces until his crushing defeat at Fredricksburg. Burnside and Ellsworth reported favorably on the Sawyer gun. Prototypes were brought to Norfolk News, Virginia and Sewell's Point for further testing, as well as mounting them on a steamship to see how they fared on water. During the testing period at Fort Monroe in 1858, Sylvanus contacted malaria, which was to plague him for the rest of life. Many tests were held throughout 1857 and 1858, but the representatives of the Department of Ordinance remained uncommitted to the idea of buying the rifled cannon from Sawyer.

1860s VARYING FORTUNES

In several letters to the Department of the Army over the next two years, Sawyer was still not able to secure a contract for buying his gun. Then in 1860, in a clear infringement of his patent, a gun produced by the Knapp Munitions Works of Pennsylvania introduced a similar rifled cannon at the Washington Navy Yard and won the government contract. Sawyer appealed to the Secretary of War, the undersecretaries of the Army and the Navy, and even to the newly-elected President Lincoln himself. Nothing came of his appeal.

In 1861 Sylvanus received a patent for a fuse hood that helped concentrate fire upon a time fuse in his cannon and then in 1862, he and his brother, Addison, were given a patent for a combination fuse. Not getting anywhere with appeals to his own federal government, Sylvanus entered into negotiations with Mexico and with the South American countries of Brazil and Chile to sell them his cannons. In Mexico, the Juarez government was preparing itself for defense against the joint British and French expeditionary force that invaded their country in 1861. Brazil had joined Argentina in its war against Paraguay, and Chile had been involved for years in an ongoing civil war between the old oligarchy and the new Liberal Republic.

The 1860s ushered in a period of tribulation for Henry and Frances Lowe. Their new daughter, Annie, born in the spring of 1860, died later that year. The following year, their only son, Charles, died of scarlet fever at the age of three. The next year, 1862, another girl, Clara, was born, but died in infancy. But happily, in February of 1864, a second son, Frank Preston Lowe, was born. Frank was to be their only son to survive into adulthood.

Henry's stomach ailments worsened as his business dropped off. In 1861, a jeweler by the name of Frank Palmer came to work in Henry's shop, and there is at least one English movement still in existence with F.L.Palmer engraved on the top plate. The federal government, in order to help finance the War of Southern Insurrection, passed tariff laws, imposing excise taxes on all imported goods. For Lowe, this meant a sharply increased cost of the watch movements he imported from England and Switzerland. Reuben Conn, who had merged Goodnow's business with his own jewelry business, was able to do this more competitively, offering better prices because of larger volume. In 1864, the federal government passed another tariff law on imported manufactured goods, making it even harder for Lowe to make a profit without charging prices that were much higher than Conn's.

Sylvanus Sawyer, meanwhile, continued to prosper in some areas while other endeavors caused him ongoing headaches. Looking forward to a potentially huge market for his cannons, he erected a new building, in 1864 and 1865, on lower Main Street on an acre of his garden property, in the same neighborhood as factories belonging to the Simonds Saw Company. Sawyer himself designed and oversaw the construction of the building which stands to this day and is currently used by Fitchburg Plumbing Supply as a warehouse and retail store. By the time the building was completed and ready for occupancy in early 1866, wars in the United States and the three other countries with which he had negotiated contracts came to an end. Sawyer gave up making cannons but retained ownership of the building in which he set up a small machine-building company to make calipers and measuring tools. The rest of the spacious building was leased to other enterprises such as C. H. Brown and Company, and the Fitchburg Machine Company, partly owned by his old friend from Templeton, Sylvester C. Wright.

Loss of the potential armament business engendered a change of plans for Sawyer, but it did not dull his ardor for the things he loved best. The innovation and the beauty of his greenhouse and gardens made him the area's foremost florist, with people coming by train from Boston and Worcester to view his varying hybrids and exotic plants. In August of 1867 he was given a patent for calipers and dividers with screw adjustments and another patent for dividers in 1868. That year saw two more patents received, one for an improved rattan-cutting machine and another for an improved steam engine.

A story is told about what could possibly have been the first automobile accident in the country, occurring in the fall of 1865, and involving Sylvanus Sawyer. There are different versions of this story, some which put Sawyer in the driver's seat and others which talk about a different Sawyer named Sylvester. Since the story is about the kind of thing Sylvanus might do, there is a good chance it is about him. Possibly reviving his old foot-pedaled hand-car ideas about alternative power for carriages, he built a wood-powered steam drive for a buckboard. With a friend, Sylvester "Skipper" Wright, he drove what was described by a bystander as a "buggy with a burning steam engine" to South Royalston, Massachusetts for a celebration in honor of the Union victory and the end of the Civil War. They drove the buggy around the town common, to the delight of all those in attendance, reaching "excessive speed"— probably no more than ten miles an hour—and crashed into a tree spilling the occupants and the steam boiler. There is no mention of whether anyone was hurt, other than possibly a bruised ego.

Henry Lowe struggled through the war economy, seeing his profits dwindle. Shortly after the war, most individual New England watchmakers were again importing movements from Europe and casing them in American-made watch cases. But they had an increasingly difficult time competing against the plethora of watches being manufactured domestically. By 1866, the American Watch Company in Waltham was producing over 30,000 watches per year. And new companies were springing up in New England and New York. Tariffs on imported manufactured goods were not lifted after the war, making it even harder for the individual watchmaker. To make matters worse, the economy had begun to slide into a post-war depression.

Lowe tried to persuade William Learned to come back and help him, but instead was convinced by Learned that if he couldn't beat the enemy, the large watch manufacturer, the best thing to do was to join him. So, in 1867, Henry Lowe, at the age of forty-five, after twenty-four years in business, let Frank Palmer go, sold his stock and trade to a James Fairbanks, and packed up his wife and four children and moved them to Jersey City, New Jersey. Frances was pregnant again and due to give birth at any time. Fortunately, she had the help of her two oldest daughters, Helen, who was twenty and Louise, who was eighteen. Both Helen and Louise balked at leaving their friends, aunts, uncles and cousins, beaus, and the wonderful Fitchburg parties, but they would never dream of abandoning their mother in her time of need, nor their father at what might be the opportunity of his lifetime.

The family traveled by train to New York City and then by ferry across the Hudson River to Jersey City where they settled into a house in Marion a few blocks from the United States Watch Company plant. They arrived just in time for Frances to give birth to the youngest daughter, Florence, in December of 1867. Frances, at age forty-four when Florence was born, was sick through much of the final term of the pregnancy and Henry was concerned about the health of the newborn child. But he took it as a good omen of happy times to come when the little girl seemed to be as healthy as her older sisters. So, the Christmas of 1867 was a happy one after all. Even though they were away from Henry and Frances's large and loving families in Fitchburg, they were facing a new adventure together.

William Learned led the new watch factory as its superintendent. He placed Lowe in the position of finish room supervisor. Lowe's health seemed to have improved with the move from Fitchburg and the release from the years of fretting over the shop on Main Street. In the finish room he could concentrate on what he liked doing most, overseeing the meticulous details involved in putting together manufactured parts into a well-running watch.

One snowy evening, not long after Henry started in his new position, he and his two daughters, Helen and Louise, possibly picked up in the Learned's open sleigh, attended a gala dinner party at the house of Fredrick Giles, the company president. Very likely, over port and cigars, with the men gathered in the library after dinner, Mr. Giles and his partner, Mr. Wales, could both have reiterated to their managers their goal for the company—to manufacture the finest watches made in America. The prospect of being given the opportunity to supervise the finishing of so wonderful a product must have excited Henry, as it would anyone who had so far spent his entire adult life concentrating on repairing and fine-tuning such a delicate instrument as a pocket watch.

The United States Watch Company lasted twelve years, from the forming of the stock company in 1864 to its reorganization in 1872 as the Marion Watch Company, and then its final demise in 1874. Sylvanus Sawyer might have been influenced by Henry J. Lowe to invest in its future. Or it could have happened the other way, with Sawyer influencing Lowe. The Putnam Machine Company had installed the steam power supply when the factory in the Marion was built, so the company was well known to the residents of Fitchburg. Sawyer understood the workings of a stock company. The United States Watch Company in 1867 looked to him like a solid investment. Giles, Wales and Company had a good reputation as jewelers and watch dealers in New York, and by the time Lowe went to work in the finish room, the first watches were being produced in the new factory building. And

Sawyer's investment in the watch company went beyond financial considerations. Ever since he had worked on repairing watches as a young man he had retained his fascination with the intricate beauty of the workings of a mechanical watch. He could never be a watchmaker himself, turning out the same thing day after day, or sit still and focus long enough to work at it for many hours at a stretch. But after all these years, he could still become excited over the plans for new watch designs, especially ones in the possession of people whose ambition it was to make the best machine-made watch in the country. He leapt at the chance to invest with Lowe's new employer. Sawyer originally invested in the New Jersey watch company in 1867 and then again in its reorganization in 1872, making him one of three major stockholders in the enterprise.

The United States Watch Company did reach Giles's goal of producing, arguably, the best American-made watch in 1871, but at a considerable cost to the owners. Frederick Giles was a stringent taskmaster. He drove his employees hard and paid them austere wages. Giles was noted for his flinty, and somewhat irascible, temperment that resulted in continual controversy between him and his employees. Early on, his design engineer, James Gerry who had come from Waltham, left after arguing with Giles. The entire history of the company was pockmarked with labor unrest and employees leaving en masse. In 1869, William Learned was removed by Giles after a year-long run of animosity. Learned sued Giles for breaking his contract and, even though it took two years in court, Learned eventually won a decision against the watch company owners.

As a result of Learned's leaving in 1869, Lowe was promoted to a position of superintendent, a job that was limited to direct supervision of manufacturing operations. Another superintendent, George Hart, supervised the development of the company's machinery and they both answered to an overall superintendendent, another of Giles's brothers-in-law, Henry Wright. Fortunately for Lowe and Hart, Wright functioned as a buffer between them and Frederick Giles.

In his position as superintendent in charge of manufacturing, Henry Lowe has been credited with making many innovative refinements to the manufacturing process. Under his direction, the United States Watch Company produced its highest grade watch, the United States Watch Company grade. The 16-size ¼-plate and bridge model, the company's finest watch, commanding the highest price of any watch in the country, was manufactured under Henry J. Lowe's direction. Unfortunately, however, financial outlay always seemed to loom larger than income for the Marion company. The nation's economy fluctuated up and down from the end of the war to the autumn of 1873, and the United States Watch Company, or Marion Watch Company as it was called by that time, had never attained a solid enough financial footing to weather the crash of 1873.

1870s OPPORTUNITY AND LOSS

The late 1860s and early 1870s were a busy time in Sawer's life. Well into his forties, he proved what his acquaintances had always suspected, that he was a confirmed bachelor. He participated fully in the social life of the city, with his brothers Addison and Joseph and their families, and with his friend Sylvester Wright. He invested money in his cousin Walter's company, the Sawyer and Esty Sewing Machine Company, and then began tinkering with ways of improving existing sewing machine designs.

Fitchburg industry, like that of the rest of the northern states, grew and expanded at a rapid rate after the economic dip in 1867. Business at the American Rattan Company was booming and Sawyer's New England Machine Company was doing very well, manufacturing calipers, dividers and other kinds of measuring instruments for watchmakers and machinists. Sawyer hired his nephew, Eden Sawyer, to manage the greenhouse and florist business. This business had become one of the most famous of its kind in New England. So much so that one person who was sure to have visited there, and most probably had learned from Sawyer was a young man from Lancaster by the name of Luther Burbank. At that time, Charles Darwin's recently published book, "The Origin of the Species" would surely have been of interest to both of them. Burbank, still in his twenties, bought his own farm in Lunenburg, a few miles away from Sawyer's greenhouse, and there developed several new breeds of vegetables, fruits, flowers and grasses just as Sawyer was doing. Burbank later sold his farm to move to California, where he eventually became world famous for his more than 800 varieties of different strains and breeds of plants.

In 1874, Sawyer suffered another financial setback. The United States Watch Company, which had become the Marion Watch Company, finally went bankrupt. The Wall Street panic of September 1873 had delivered a crushing blow for the Marion investment as well as for many companies in Fitchburg. Sawyer took a substantial loss at the United States Watch Company but, on a trip to New Jersey, he did manage to negotiate with Giles for the acquisition of certain watchmaking tools and equipment to partially compensate him. Upon advice from Henry J. Lowe, the first choice of equipment would be the machines for the manufacture of the 16 size, ¼-plate and bridge movement. Very likely, it was on this trip to New Jersey that he convinced Lowe to move his family back to Fitchburg and help him set up another watchmaking enterprise.

Sawyer, however, found himself in tight financial straits for the first time in many years. He was already in the process of erecting a new, very large, rotary greenhouse which was finished in December of 1875. Orders for measurement instruments had dropped off with the economic downturn. The rattan company was showing a deep slide in profits for the first time since opening its doors more than thirty years before. Negotiations were underway to sell the company to the Wakefield Rattan Company. Cyrus Wakefield, who had been a minor shareholder from the beginning, bought out all the remaining shares. The company was eventually moved to Gardener, Massachusetts to form the Heywood-Wakefield Furniture Company.

In April of 1875 Lowe brought his family back to Fitchburg, all except for Helen and Louise, both of whom had married. Louise, married to Chauncey Mason, a watch company employee, had two children, Nellie and a second daughter, Florence, named after her sister who had died two months before of scarlet fever. Helen was married to a Henry Nason, also a watch company employee, but there were no children as yet. Jennie Maria, at age seventeen, and Frank, who would be nine that summer, moved back with their parents to a house on Green Street in Fitchburg owned by Henry's brother who lived next door.

With bankruptcy and reorganization of the Marion Watch Company, several employees left and went with Lowe back to Fitchburg. These were mostly skilled machinists, many of whom, such as Gilmore Crowell, William Guest, A.R. Bardeen, and Charles Dodge, had originally come from Massachusetts. They followed Lowe with the promise of finding employment in a new watch manufacturing venture in Fitchburg.

The Lowe family remained devastated by the death of the little girl, Florence. She was eight years old and had been the joy of Henry's and Frances' lives. Later that year, Helen returned to Fitchburg to give birth to her first child who was named Fannie. In the fall of 1875, Henry contacted tuberculosis—at that time called consumption—which weakened him more and more over the next year until he finally died in August of 1876. His extended obituary in the *Fitchburg Sentinel* cited, as his major accomplishment in life, the many happy customers of his watchmaking business who still proudly "own watches made by him" in his shop at Main and Central Street. This is obviously an error on the part of the obituary writer as no watch with Lowe's name on it, other than on a watch paper, has ever come to light. More than likely, what the reporter was referring to were the many movements that Henry purchased, put into cases, and then retailed. However, from a present-day perspective, it can be said that the major accomplishment of Lowe's life was the manufacture of one watch, the rarest of American specimens, the Fitchburg Watch, the only single "mass-produced" watch ever made.

With the sale of the American Rattan Company, Sylvanus Sawyer's substantial yearly income from his stock holdings in the company came to an end. He received a share of money from the sale that he calculated would just about allow him to live comfortably into his old age. Meanwhile, his cousin's sewing machine company was doing a little better with improvements Sylvanus had made, for which he was granted another patent in 1877.

The florist business held its own, making a profit year after year, especially with the new greenhouse that could be rotated to follow the movement of the sun from morning till evening. He also designed and had built a new seventy-two foot one-story brick building for potting and storage. Train tours were booked regularly from Boston and Worcester bringing groups of horticultural mavens out to view his plants. He grew eight different varieties of hothouse grapes plus hardy strains of strawberries, cucumbers, mushrooms and tomatoes. Inside the greenhouse were lemon trees, orange trees, and banana trees, as well as pineapples growing in pots, coconut and fan palms, Brazilian ferns and many breeds of hybrid azaleas, camellias, calla lilies and japonicas.

With the help of many votes from The Patch, Sawyer was elected alderman of the seventh ward, the section that included lower Main Street, in 1877. As an alderman, he increased his efforts for the clean-up of the Nashua River. The battle to establish a sewer system had still not been won against the more conservative voters of the city who felt there was no reason not to continue dumping the city sewage into the river as they had always done. The residents of The Patch, as well as Sawyer himself, still fought the battle mainly against the stench of the river, but there was growing evidence that the sewage was at fault for the cholera, typhus, scarlet fever, and tuberculosis epidemics which wiped out a significant percentage of the city's children every few years.

When Henry J. Lowe died in August of 1876, his son Frank, at age eleven, was the only minor child left at home. It is not unlikely that Frank went to work in the fledgling watch factory, which would have helped further his teaching in Henry's trade for which he seems to have shown an aptitude. Frank married Rosa Nell Wright, the daughter of Sylvanus' friend Sylvester, and worked for two years at Sylvester's Fitchburg Machine Company before taking a position as assistant job master in one of the train-making departments of the Waltham Watch Company. He passed the Fitchburg Watch on to his son, Carroll Henry Lowe, who also grew up to work at the Waltham company, and from whose widow's estate, Fred Selchow acquired the watch.

Henry's widow Frances moved back to the Thurston household on Mechanic Street in the winter of 1877, after she herself took ill. In February 1878, while visiting her daughter Louise in Marion, New Jersey, she also died of tuberculosis.

In the months after Frances' death, Sylvanus Sawyer seemed to lose the will to go on. He ended his efforts to raise money for the limping watch company and went into semi-retirement in his home on Summer Street. He gave up his seat as alderman and spent his time puttering in his greenhouse. His cousin Adelaide Sawyer, the daughter of Uncle Joseph from Royalston, kept house for him. Her sister Mary, a close friend of Frances Thurston Lowe, who had been a painter of fine portraits, also came to live in the Summer Street mansion. Perhaps it was the care of these two women that revived Sylvanus' will to plunge into his next endeavor the following year.

THOMAS PALMER

One other person who deserves credit in the formation of the watch company of Fitchburg is Dr. Thomas Palmer. A very successful local dentist and a founding member of the Fitchburg Board of Trade, Palmer headed the board's committee that studied the feasibility of the watch company venture. What he and the committee found not only led him to an enthusiastic advocacy for the new company, but also to getting in line right behind Sylvanus Sawyer to invest his own money.

The new companies set up by the Board of Trade were not the first investments Palmer had made in an effort to stimulate both business and culture in his hometown. He was well known for his open hand, and could very likely have been the first person Sawyer approached with the idea of funding the new company. Palmer was two years older than Sawyer and Lowe and had already made his fortune by his mid-thirties. Born in 1820 in No Town, he began his practice of dentistry in Fitchburg in 1843 and not only conducted the largest practice in the area, but ran a dental school as well. His son, Joseph, joined him and continued the practice well into the 20th century, after Thomas's death in 1907.

After hearing a lecture by a certain Dr. Fowler, a phrenologist, on the positive aspects of octagon-shaped buildings, which provided their inhabitants with much more light and air, Thomas Palmer designed and had built such a house for his practice and dental school on Main

Street. As carpenters erected the building, they were paid at the end of each day from proceeds of that day's dental business. The building, an octagonal, three-storied structure, was completed in 1848. The unusual shape prompted Daniel Webster, who was campaigning in Fitchburg for Zachary Taylor, to comment that "it would make a good churn, if only it had a dash," meaning that it looked like a butter churn without the handle showing from the top.

Palmer seems to have come by his intelligence and hs eccentricities as an inheritance from his father, also named Joseph Palmer. The elder Joseph owned a farm in the area called No Town, because it was not claimed by any of the neighboring towns of Leominster and Fitchburg, nor by the town of Sterling to the south. Prior to the coming of the railroad, one branch of the Massachusetts Turnpike ran across his property, for which he legally collected tolls from every wagon and coach traveling east or west. In the 1840s, his idealism led him to throw in with the Transcendentalist, Bronson Alcott, helping him to establish a Utopian community called Fruitlands in what is now Harvard, Massachusetts. The community failed after the first year and the land was sold to Palmer who worked it for thirty years, realizing a very decent profit.

An interesting story is told about old Joseph Palmer who maintained a copious beard at a time when beards were not in fashion. On the front porch of a Main Street hotel in Fitchburg three gentlemen accosted him with the intention of shaving his face. Announcing loudly that Jesus himself wore a beard, Joseph defended himself against the attack. The other men were cut so badly by his knife that he was taken to court and ordered to pay a fine. Refusing to pay the fine, which he claimed to be immoral because he had only acted to defend himself, he was sentenced to jail where he languished for a year and a half until the court finally relented and released him without collecting the fine.

Both Thomas Palmer's practice, as well as the dental school, enjoyed a considerable success, partially due to his forward-thinking acceptance of new technology. In 1845, he was invited by Dr. William T.G. Morton to view the use of ether in performing surgery. Morton later furnished Palmer with an inhaler allowing him to begin using ether in his dental practice in 1846, making him one of the very first pioneers in the use of anesthesia in dentistry. The first person to benefit from the use of ether in having a tooth pulled was a Mr. Ebenezer Hopkins Frost, a music teacher from Groton, Massachusetts. In November of 1846, Palmer took the breathing apparatus down to the Baltimore Dental College, the only such professional dental school in the country at the time, and demonstrated it to the faculty, administrating the gas to a slave who, after having his tooth pulled, reported feeling no pain. Palmer appears in a commemorative group photo, along with his son, Morton's widow, and several other medical pioneers at Massachusetts General Hospital on what was, and is still known as "Ether Day" in 1896, the 50th anniversary of its first use.

It is true that Thomas Palmer, like several other founding members and supporters of the Fitchburg Board of Trade, was not an industrialist per se, but it was his kind of generosity and civic spirit that formed the impetus behind the Board of Trade. It was his kind of creative thinking, shared with Sylvanus Sawyer and others in the city, that prompted the establishment of the watch company.

Photo courtesy of Fitchburg Historical Society

Dr. Thomas Palmer

146

Top plate engraving on The Fitchburg Watch

Chapter 7

THE COMPANY

The most likely reason the watch company of Fitchburg existed at all was that it represented the potential realization of a dream of Sylvanus Sawyer's. He had a love of beauty, as evidenced by the many flowers he developed in his greenhouses, as well as a love of mechanics that he worked with, theorized about, improved upon, or just tinkered with all his life. He also seems to have had a passion for precise measurement, as shown by his many patents for calipers and other machinists' measuring devices. What endeavor could be more apt in combining these three passions of beauty, mechanics, and precision as the opportunity to produce a pocket watch of the same quality as those made by the company in which he had recently invested so much money, the United States Watch Company.

This passion is what led Sawyer to invest in the United States Watch Company to begin with, then to take possession of that company's best watch machine tools when they went bankrupt, and then to convince the Fitchburg Board of Trade to sponsor the start-up of the new company. He invested his own money, worked diligently to attract other investors, and abandoned his efforts only when there was finally no hope of carrying on. We can only think that, like Giles and Wales of the United States Watch Company, his desire for making a fine watch outdistanced his ordinarily good sense in money matters.

No records of the watch company of Fitchburg are known to exist. It is possible, though, to establish a definition of the company, know something of its workings, and make some educated assumptions on what happened inside the company itself. Cosmologists have never been able to actually view black holes in space, but they can determine their existence, and know a great deal about them by observing what goes on around the outside of that most elusive physical phenomenon. In the same manner, even though there is no direct window into what actually happened inside the watch company, local newspaper stories and Board of Trade reports give an outline sketch that can be filled in to form a fairly accurate picture.

The economic conditions of the 1870s provided not only the background for the establishment of the watch company, but also the reason for its failure. When Fitchburg incorporated as a city in 1872, its future looked nothing but rosy. With the influx of immigration, the population had grown to over 12,000. The first water mains were installed with fire hydrants strategically located near each industrial center in the city. Sewage, though, was still being emptied into the Nashua River. Fitchburg's industry—paper, textile, furniture, steam engine, cutting tools, and machine tools— outpaced the country as a whole with an optimistic 6% expansion each year since the middle of the Civil War. By the 1870s Fitchburg had become the world leader in the production of cross-cut saws, and steel horse collars, and was the United States leader in producing boilers and brass castings.

But industrial and economic growth changed drastically when, beginning with the Panic of 1873, the country was thrown into the worst depression it had suffered up to that time. First signs of economic difficulties could be seen with the fall of the Berlin stock market in 1872 in the aftermath of the recently-fought Franco-Prussian War. The shock wave created a domino effect in Vienna, Brussels, Paris and London. The resultant depression dried up the major founts of venture capital for United States industrialists, and shriveled the market for American products. The American economy held steady throughout the winter and the summer of 1873, but the cash shortage of over-extended railroads and, with the federal government's war debt coming due, a September panic forced the closing of Wall Street and the failure of several leading banks and investment firms. Two weeks after the September closing, the stock market recovered slightly, but ushered in an economic downturn second only to that of the 1930s. The manufacturing whirlwind was over, and the companies still intact after the resultant shake-down of the next five years were only those that had already attained an industrial and financial maturity.

The watchmaking industry, except for the Elgin company which was still paying dividends, was as hard hit as other industries. The American Waltham Watch

Company, while still producing an average of 100,000 watches a year, struggled mightily through the depression years. Elsewhere, the Empire Watch Company, an attempt by the former United States/Marion Watch Company to recover from bankruptcy, folded in 1877. The depression became a factor in the closings of the Cornell/California Watch Company, the Rock Island Watch Company, the Washington Watch Company, the New York Watch Company, the Adams and Perry Watch Company, and the Freeport Watch Company. And only re-organization, plus an additional infusion of funds from the community, kept the Illinois Springfield Watch Company alive.

As a reaction to the lack of available money to people for the purchase of even mid-range watch grades, the year 1877 saw the beginning of two companies dedicated to the production of low-cost watches. The Auburndale Watch Company failed in its attempt to make an affordable watch within the first year and then focused on stopwatches and timers for the rest of their short history. In Waterbury, Connecticut, the Benedict and Burnham Manufacturing Company, using inexpensively produced machinery and unskilled labor, finally made a success of producing cheap watches.

Throughout the fall and into the winter of 1873, Fitchburg industry felt the increasing pinch of constricted markets. Machine orders dropped off, textile and paper warehouses filled with unshipped products, and accounts receivable remained unpaid. Mills were idled and workers laid off. The rosy future, envisioned at the city's incorporation ceremony only a year ago, had begun to wilt. And the news from Boston, New York and Washington signaled more of the same, if not worse. In 1874, industrial leaders of Fitchburg celebrated the opening of the Hoosac Tunnel which linked the city by rail to the west, but their excitement was short lived as shipments of raw materials and finished products dropped off to well below earlier pre-tunnel levels.

The reaction in Fitchburg to the economic downturn was to band together. Crocker, Simonds, Miles, Lawrence, Wallace, and other industrial leaders were not the kind of men to deal with adversity by hunkering down until it blew over. Civic feeling ran high. Fitchburg was an industrial city, a tight-knit community whose livelihood was dependent on its industry. In January of 1874, after four months of seeing which way the economic winds were blowing, they formed the Fitchburg Board of Trade. The new board's first meeting was dedicated to paying honor to the memory of Alvah Crocker, the city's leading industrialist, who had passed away between Christmas and New Year's Day. Rodney Wallace, president of the Fitchburg Paper Company was elected as the board's first President and George Simonds, president of Simonds Manufacturing, and the father of a future superintendent of the Waltham Watch Company, was elected Secretary. Sylvanus Sawyer, Thomas Palmer, and three of Henry J. Lowe's brothers were among the founding members. Their first order of business was to do something about what was the potentially devastating debt that had been accrued by the Worcester North Agricultural Society, an organization of farmers in northern Worcester County that provided most of the food consumed by the city. Several other city businesses also received help from the Board of Trade.

By January of 1875, the membership of the Board of Trade had grown to 173. On April 5 of that same year, Sylvanus Sawyer made a presentation before the board for the potential success of starting a watch manufacturing business in the city. He gave a lengthy and detailed account of the watchmaking industry in the United States since 1850, citing the world-wide prestige that such communities as Waltham, Massachusetts and Elgin, Illinois had gained from hosting these businesses. He broke down for the board a cost analysis of a watch factory, showing expenses and potential revenues for the subscribers. Machine tools, he said, were 50 percent of a watch factory's expense, stock was 8 to 10 percent. He compared this with expenses in his own firm, the American Rattan Company, where machine tools accounted for 53 percent and stock was as high as 25 percent. In the lean times of the recent economic downturn, expenses for salaries and factory space were highly negotiable and could be controlled to reflect decent profits for the investors, and for re-investing in the company.

Sylvanus gave an overly-optimistic estimate of a time schedule for tooling up, four to six months to have the machines ready to begin making watches. He stated also that he was already in possession of three pieces of high-quality watch tool machinery, obtained from the recently bankrupted United States/Marion Watch Company. The creative talent for the designing and making of the watches themselves already existed in the person of Henry J. Lowe. A committee on manufacturing, including Charles Crocker, George Spencer, J.L. Chapman, and James Phillips was appointed to study the feasibility of starting a firm to manufacture watches.

The findings of the committee led to a determination that, as an industrial pursuit, the manufacture of watches had a lot to be said for it. Companies like American Waltham, Howard, and Elgin seemed to have the ability to survive even in a fluctuating economy. There was no necessity for a large outlay of capital for raw material or transportation of material in or out of the plant. The men who made watches tended to be, in their terms, a better class of citizen, more intelligent, better read, and more "gentlemanly" than the average factory worker. And, once the watch-making machinery was set up, it could be operated by people who had previously learned manufacturing skills in very different types of factories, such as textile or paper mills.

Not only would a watch factory enhance the city's economic growth, it would add prestige to the community. Such was the reputation that the watch industry enjoyed in the relatively new American industrial climate of the late nineteenth century. Citizens of Fitchburg, just as in communities like Springfield, Illinois and Berkeley, California, appeared willing to invest, and sometimes donate, funds or services to have such a fashionable item as a fine pocket watch made in, and named after, their town. In an era when mechanics was king, groups of railroad men sat around their lunch pails, comparing the jeweling of each other's watch, bank officers started meetings by checking the accuracy of each other's glittering timepiece, and industrial leaders perked up at the chance to tell people that one of the best little machines in the world was made right there in their own home town.

At the April 19 meeting, the committee to obtain subscriptions for the watch factory, led by Thomas Palmer, gave a very favorable report. In their opinion, the board needed to raise $75,000 to launch the project. It is difficult to know on what specifics this figure is based, as it seems to have been an extremely conservative estimate. A more realistic capitalization would have been $150,000 to support a factory for two years before it could begin bringing in a profit. However, there could have been several reasons why such a low appraisal was given to the board. It may be that the committee kept the goal of $75,000 purposely low in order to make it seem more attainable to potential investors in a time of economic hardship. With Sylvanus Sawyer's time estimate of six months to build machinery, they could have looked forward to the watch company returning a profit within one year. Those on the Board of Trade were so filled with enthusiasm about the project of the watch company that they grossly over-estimated what they could do as well as under-estimated what they needed to get it done.

At any rate, half of $75,000 had already been pledged by Sylvanus Sawyer, Thomas Palmer and others. A Dr. Fisher, one of the board members, asked where all the watches being made would go; would there be a market for them? A Mr. Lawrence from New York City, "a gentleman of large experience in the manufacture and sale of watches, replied that millions of dollars were annually expended in this country for foreign watches, and all that is necessary to secure this trade for American companies is the manufacture of first-class watches equal to the Swiss or other foreign makes." He had examined the designs for the new watch as well as the machinery already obtained by Sawyer and declared them to be as good as, and in some cases superior to, anything he had seen coming from Europe. He had no doubt that the "home and foreign demand for American watches would afford ample market for all the first-class watches the proposed factory could turn out."

Sylvanus then spoke to members again, saying that "the impression seemed to prevail with some that he wished to have the factory here so as to afford him a position as manager or director, but he disclaimed any such object; he had abundant business…he had carried the enterprise thus far because he had faith it could be made a successful business and add materially to the prosperity of the city." Dr. Fisher stated that he had previously subscribed for stock in the company and, after investigating the matter to his own satisfaction, he would double his investment. Then Mr. Sawtell, the board's recording secretary, spoke of the superior literary and moral standing of the workmen at the Waltham Watch Company and hoped that the new factory scheduled for Fitchburg might "afford an opening for an excellent class of mechanics, as well as furnishing large dividends for those who invest in the stock."

On April 26, Sylvanus gave another presentation in which he informed the members that American-made watches had recently competed successfully at a show in Vienna with some of the best watches made in Europe. As to the new company, he proposed that it would be under the direction of Henry J. Lowe, as superintendent. He showed that the cost of building tools to make five watches per day would be the same as to make 20 watches a day. Eugene Miles, president of Whitman & Miles and current mayor of Fitchburg, made an enthusiastic announcement, offering a building owned by him on Farwell Place for housing the factory. The building measured 60 by 40 feet, had two stories and an attic as well as an engine and fuel room measuring 12 by 40 feet. The building was equipped with a Campbell & Whittier, one cylinder, six horsepower, steam engine. Miles offered the building free of rent, and with taxes and insurance paid by his company for two years. After that, he would want a lease for five years at $600 per year. The board voted in favor of sponsoring the watch factory, recommending that they lease the building as opposed to building their own, and that they limit their output to five watches a day and increase production as the demand for the watches increased.

The Board of Trade's meeting, on June 8, was held at the shop where watch tool machinery was in various stages of completion. They had, at present, 22 lathes that were being built, each at a cost of about $150. In addition, the company had the three lathes that had been brought up from the old United States/Marion Watch Company, worth $250 each. The total number of employees at that time was eight, three of whom were non-producing, including Henry J. Lowe, as superintendent, and Gilmer Crowell, as shop foreman. The six other employees were William Guest, who later served for a short time as superintendent of the Auburndale Watch Company, Charles Whitehouse, A.R. Bardeen, Charles Vanderhoff, Thomas Parker, and Charles Dodge. All eight of these men had previously worked for the United States/Marion Watch Company.

Sylvanus gave a presentation wherein he revised the financial and time-schedule estimates of what was needed to be operational. They would require from seven to eight months for completing the machinery at a total cost of $100,000, revised up from $75,000. He assured the board that when the machinery was complete, they would be able to produce watches superior to anything then made, at less cost than what was presently required to make a first-class watch. The design for the new watch, he said, would be better than anything either Waltham or Elgin had produced so far. It was similar to the best watch made by the United States Watch Company. As the company advanced into full production they would need 60 employees to manufacture 15 to 20 watches per day. These men should be able to produce one watch for a cost of about $30, but, once they were in full production, they could produce 15 watches for $10 each. Sylvanus went on to say that he had engaged a man from New York City who was certain he could sell all their watches.

George Simonds then got up and spoke in favor of the watch company's potential success, as did John Haskins, board member and president of Haskins Machine Company. Haskins said that he could see the watch company's arc of increased production similar to that of his own company. When he had first come to Fitchburg to build steam engines, he produced three engines the first year. The second year he built 30 engines, with 115 in the third year.

At the next monthly meeting of the Board of Trade, on July 12, a committee was appointed for the purpose of securing subscribers to invest in the new watch company. Sylvanus led the committee that included Amasa Norcross, the previous mayor of Fitchburg, Rodney Wallace, Eugene Miles, Gardner Burbank, co-owner of the Crocker Burbank Paper Company, H.F. Coggshall, and J.W. Kimball, a sampling of the most influential industrialists in the city. At the September meeting, Dr. Thomas Palmer joined the committee, replacing Sylvanus as its chairman, and began to spearhead efforts to interest investors. Palmer, J.M. Harris, and David Boutelle all offered land on which to begin building a factory to house the watch company. It was suggested that Boutelle's land on Myrtle Avenue would be the most appropriate. Palmer and Sylvanus were the major subscribers. Five of the watch company's employees, Lowe, Crowell, Guest, Vanderhoff, and Whitehouse all invested money. The other investors included the two Goodrich brothers, George Colony, Michael Kilvan who supervised Sylvanus' New England Machine Company, John Haskins, Fred Fosdick, president of the Fitchburg Steam Engine Company, A.B. Sherman, A.W. Sydney, and I.C. Wright.

One very important piece of information about the watch company of Fitchburg that is uncertain today is the actual name of the company. Crossman referred to it as the Fitchburg Watch Company. From the publication of his articles in the 1880s until Fred Selchow's discovery of the prototype watch in 1968, all references to the company called it the Fitchburg Watch Company. After Selchow uncovered the watch with "Union Watch Company" engraved on the top plate, he and other knowledgeable collectors and museum curators began referring to the company in their literature as the Union Watch Company. Their argument runs that, since Sawyer and/or Lowe went so far as to engrave the name on the top plate, then it must have been their intention to name the company thus. There is no other reference, previous to Selchow, to the company being called the Union Watch Company.

There is, however, one other reference, besides Crossman's, to the company's name to be found in a newspaper article in the *Fitchburg Reveille*, dated October 10, 1875. A meeting had been held to work out the arrangements for filing corporation papers to be filed with the Commonwealth of Massachusetts. The article gives the list of attendees: Thomas Palmer, Sylvanus Sawyer, George Angell, W. H. Guest, H.A. Goodrich, George D. Colony, Michael Kivlon, John Haskins, Fred Fosdick, and Henry Piper. The article went on to explain that up to that point capital stock amounting to $50,000 had been obtained, and the desired goal in selling shares was to raise capital equaling $150,000. Five hundred shares would be issued to sell for $100 each. The article also stated that the committee decided at the meeting that incorporation papers would be filed giving the new stock company the name "Fitchburg Watch Company." However, there is no record in the Massachusetts state house of these corporation papers ever being filed.

Is it possible that Crossman, in calling the company the Fitchburg Watch Company, got his information from this newspaper article? Possibly. A more likely scenario, though, given the other details he reported about the company, is that he got his information from someone living at the time who was knowledgeable about the facts of the company. And Crossman has always been held to be quite credible in the details put into his articles about the watch manufacturing companies compiled in his book.

The company name is a conundrum. On the one hand, there is a name engraved in the top plate of the company's only known watch. That fact is irrefutable. On the other hand, there are two references in ink to the name Fitchburg Watch Company. Having it clearly stated that the intention of the committee—and therefore the Fitchburg Board of Trade itself—to found the watch company and name it after their city, it is difficult to imagine them opting for a name so vague and nondescript as "Union." That name might be conceivably appropriate in 1864 during the war between the Union and the Confederacy, but in the middle 1870s, the name was sure to have lost its fervor. Sylvanus Sawyer's dream notwithstanding, the company was formed by men filled with civic pride. In the throes of a deep financial depression, these men, known locally as the "Fitchburg Hustlers," bound and determined to pull their little clearing-in-the-woods up by its own bootstraps, would have foremost in their hearts a name that would reflect their home town. Even if it is not known exactly what the company was called, there are some probabilities that lend themselves toward the name Fitchburg Watch Company.

In the middle of the nineteenth century most watch manufacturing firms, like other types of industries, were named after either their location or their owner: Nashua, Tremont, Melrose, Newark, Freeport, on the one hand, or Appleton Tracy, E. Howard, Cornell, Mozart, Adams & Perry on the other. And there were a few companies, named originally with a broader name, which then became localized: American Watch Company became American Waltham Watch Company, National Watch Company became Elgin National Watch Company, United States Watch Company became Marion Watch Company, Illinois Springfield became Springfield Illinois.

A similar, and very likely scenario, might have occurred with the Fitchburg company. The Fitchburg watch was most likely manufactured and engraved sometime between the company's start-up in April of 1875 and the incorporation meeting in October of that same year. One of the first orders of business in the new company would be making a prototype watch. For two reasons: (1) to help the machinists know what kind of piece they are building machinery for, and (2) to have a model to show to prospective investors. It is most probable that the prototype watch would have been finished under the supervision of, if not actually finished by the hand of, Henry J. Lowe himself, the man whose son became the owner of the watch. He would have made the watch before he became too sick to do so. By the time of the October, 1875 meeting he had fallen ill with tuberculosis, then sank lower into the clutches of that disease throughout the ensuing months, until his death in August of the following year. It is entirely possible that someone— Sawyer, Lowe, or even Palmer— had decided on the name "Union Watch Company" initially and had it engraved on the top plate. The gentlemen on the Fitchburg Board of Trade on the other hand may have wanted the organization founded and funded under their sponsorship, to proudly bear the name of their city.

We will probably never know whether the over-riding intent was to name the company the Fitchburg Watch Company or the Union Watch Company. The one thing we do know for sure is that the only known watch made by this company bears the inscription "Union Watch Company." The other thing we can surmise, given the workmanship and materials that went into this watch, is that it must have been a labor of love for Henry J. Lowe. It was under Lowe's term as superintendent of the United States Watch Company that what was considered the apogee in American watchmaking was achieved in 1871. Their top grade watch, known as the "United States Watch Company" grade was listed at a retail price of $450, at a time when the top-of-the-line Waltham or Elgin sold for $125. And here in his hometown of Fitchburg, in possession of the machinery used to create the quarter-plate and bridge movement, he had the opportunity to build what he possibly hoped would be one of the finest watches in the country.

At the November and December meetings of the Board of Trade, the subject of the watch company was not discussed. They must have known at this point that Henry J. Lowe, the creative energy behind the watch company's product, had contracted tuberculosis. Lowe's disease, one that struck fear in the hearts of anyone living in the nineteenth century, could very easily have created concern, as the vagaries of the stock market can attest, among existing and potential subscribers to invest further in the company. At any rate, it looked like investment money was going elsewhere. The November meeting concerned itself with a new potential start-up, that of a fast-loom mill. Charles Chapman, of Fitchburg, had recently been granted a patent for a loom that made suspender webbing, increasing production from an average of 15 yards per day to 100 yards per day. $40,000 was needed for initial investment, of which $25,000 was pledged within the first few minutes of the meeting.

The economic condition of the country as a whole, as well as that of Fitchburg in particular, continued to worsen as winter set in. On New Year's Day, 1876, the watch company hosted an open house. Sylvanus filled the shop with flowers from his greenhouses. Employees mixed with Board of Trade members and their wives, all toasting the success of the watch manufacturing venture. At the third annual meeting of the Board of Trade, on January 16, the first meeting to be held in the board's new hall in the Post Office Block, the membership rolls showed an increase to 250 people, including Henry J. Lowe himself. He attended the function in an effort to show prospective investors that he remained a viable force behind the potential success of the company. Efforts were made by the entire group to put a positive face on fearful economic conditions facing them that winter. L.D. Bartlett of the Putnam Machine Company gave a talk on the various types of machines and their relationship to Fitchburg's industrial and economic well-being. Many reports were read. The Agricultural Society was doing well. The reports from the

Manufacturing Committees showed the progress of efforts on behalf of the watch company and the Chapman fast-loom company.

Both economic conditions and Henry J. Lowe's health continued to worsen as the year 1876 drew on. Henry grew weaker and weaker and was able to attend to the watch factory less and less. Gilmer Crowell took over as superintendent. Thomas Palmer led an unflagging effort to raise further money from existing subscribers and to attract new ones, but to no avail. No new investment money came in and three of the machinists, Bardeen, Dodge, and Parker left to find employment elsewhere. By June, Lowe was completely bedridden, and in August he died. By the end of the year, three more employees were gone, Whitehouse, Guest, who went to work at the new Auburndale Watch Company in Weston, Massachusetts, and Crowell, who was hired by Don Mozart's old New York Manufacturing Company, which had become Hampden Watch Company in Springfield, Massachusetts. Charles Vanderhoff was the only machinist remaining, helped most likely by casual laborers from Sylvanus Sawyer's other operations.

Sylvanus, meanwhile, when not helping Palmer raise money for the watch company, spread himself out, as usual, with other interests. To cope with decreasing income from its rattan products, the American Rattan Company merged finally with the Wakefield Rattan Company, with whom it had had a close relationship since the beginning, and whom it had relied on for imports of raw cane. The completion of Sylvanus' rotary greenhouse, which was turned by a steam-powered engine to follow the movement of the sun, helped expand his flower business. And he was given a patent in 1876 for an improvement on the sole used on sewing machines manufactured by his nephew, S.W. Sawyer.

The year 1877 began, as one local commentator called it, "the darkest the city had ever known." Factories stood idle. Financially less stable businesses folded. The population decreased with laid-off workers leaving for better prospects elsewhere. The American Rattan Company's factory on Newton Lane closed and the operation merged with the Wakefield Rattan Company in Gardner, Massachusetts. Eugene Miles, the owner of the building on Farwell Place, died suddenly of a heart attack at age 50. The two years of free rent were over and the watch company, having no money to pay for a lease, moved its equipment, most likely to 1 Main Street. This building, on Sylvanus' property, was a small factory building housing another of Sylvanus' ventures, the New England Machine Company. Charles Vanderhoff left the company sometime in that year, and further work on the watch tool machinery came to a halt.

At the annual meeting of the Board of Trade in January of 1878, the subject of their sponsorship of the watch company was brought up again by Thomas Palmer and Sylvanus Sawyer. They made another pitch for subscribers, but none were forthcoming. The board did, however, agree to appoint a committee to study the viability of the venture. In the February meeting, the committee reported back to the board that, in their opinion, the watch company effort was a lost cause. The *Fitchburg Sentinel* ran as a headline to the story Sylvanus' desperate plea, "Who Will Take the Watch Company?" But no one could be convinced to hazard further money on a company that, at that point, would have to reorganize from the starting point, especially in the persistently dour financial climate still gripping the country. As far as the Board of Trade was concerned, the subject of the watch company was put to rest for the final time in February of 1878.

So, the watch company of Fitchburg existed officialy for two years and eleven months, from April of 1875 to February of 1878. Since the company could not exist financially without the auspices of the Fitchburg Board of Trade, it is highly doubtful that Sylvanus carried on, even in his own fantasies, about manufacturing such a fine watch. His dream had more than likely died a year and a half earlier with Henry J. Lowe.

It is not known whether or not the Fitchburg Watch was kept by Henry J. Lowe and passed down to his son. By rights, it should have belonged to Sylvanus Sawyer, or even to the Fitchburg Board of Trade. A watch of similar description is mentioned in Henry's will, a gold hunter case with nickel movement. It was valued in the will at $125, which would be an expensive watch for that time, about the same as a half year's salary for a laborer. The assessed value of $125 could likely have been put on the watch, that being the price of the best Waltham or Elgin, but in reality it was so unique as to have nothing for comparison. The watch was left to his wife, Frances, who in turn left it in her will to her son, Frank, when she died in January of 1878. It's also possible that the watch in the will was something different, maybe Henry's own everyday pocket watch, which, as a watchmaker all his life and superintendent of a watch factory, would naturally be a top quality timepiece. If that is the case, then it would be conceivable that Sylvanus himself bestowed the watch on the son after the company went under. Either way, Frank ended up with this beautiful watch which he passed down to his grandson, the husband of Clara Lowe.

Throughout the spring and summer of 1878, the economy showed signs of recovering, but it was too late for the watch company. In 1879, the economy of both the nation and the Fitchburg area revived. Sawyer had on his hands an idled stock of various watch tool machines and no one to finish building them, or to run them once they were capable of turning out watch parts. He wanted to make watches, but would settle for the next best thing, making the tools to make the watches. He put some of the equipment that had been made by the watch company on the market and found a few buyers. This success led to the continued manufacture of watch tools. In July of 1880, Sawyer enticed Gilmer Crowell back from Springfield, along with Charles Whitehouse. With the two of them and Michael Kilvan, he merged his new endeavor with his other company, the New England Machine Company, and formed the Sawyer Watch Tool Machine Company in the building on lower Main Street. They began to manufacture watch tool machinery in earnest. Sawyer, once again, pulled himself away from his beloved greenhouses and threw himself into working out problems in machine tool design.

Sawyer was quoted, in the *Fitchburg Sentinel*, as saying that he was hiring unskilled apprentices for his new endeavor because they had nothing to unlearn and so could start fresh with the watch tool designs. Such a statement didn't make any more sense then than it does now, but indicates that he was hiring those people he could get at the lowest wages. By December there were 12 full time employees. The same article in the *Sentinel* went on to say that it "would require 25 men to manufacture machinery as fast as ordered." It is very likely that one of the apprentices taken on at the company was Henry J. Lowe's young son, Frank Preston Lowe, who was thirteen at the time. Frank later left Fitchburg and went to work for the Waltham Watch Company, taking with him skills related to watch tool machinery he had learned before leaving Fitchburg. The most likely place for him to learn those skills was the Sawyer Watch Tool Machine Company.

Even though Sawyer had not actually been involved so much in the day-to-day management of the watch company, or the work of making the tools, he could not help tinkering with the designs of the tools themselves. This had been his pattern with every company in which he had been involved since his early days with the rattan company. After the experience of the last few years, in which he probably spent hours studying the watch company's new machinery, he would have picked up a fair amount of expertise on watch tool technology. On October 7, 1879, Sylvanus was given a patent for an attachment to a self-centering watchmakers' lathe, using a safety center pin patented earlier that year by two gentlemen named Smith and Kesselmire of Ohio. Sawyer intended to make this improvement a specialty of the new watch tool company.

The company manufactured a machine that would turn out 2,000 screws a day, screws made within a 100th of an inch diameter, with 240 threads per inch. In total, they produced 75 different types of tools and fixtures. Five sizes of lathes were manufactured, all with hollow spindles and spring chucks, as well as double taper bearings made of hardened steel, which ran with less friction than other types of bearings. They made machines for cutting teeth in small pinions, and automatic leaf polishers designed for polishing

169

the leaf and teeth of pinions. This type of cutting machine rotated the pinion itself, polishing the teeth in succession. It could be set to make a determined number of strokes per tooth for the exact number of teeth, thereby avoiding the danger of polishing a tooth the second time, thus causing an imperfection in the pinion. Their automatic staff and pivot turning machine could be set to produce staffs or pivots of exact size, straight, tapered, or with squared shoulders. It could automatically do the turning while the operator was setting up for the next piece of work, thereby saving a great deal of time.

In the year 1880, at the 13th annual exhibition of the Mechanics Benevolent Association in Boston, the company won the highest award for innovative design for the attachments on their watchmakers' lathe. In 1881, Sawyer incorporated the company. The watch tool company prospered. Some of their customers included the newly formed Western Watch Company, the Holler Chronometer Company, Auburndale Watch Company, Halls' Safe and Lock Company, E.H. Flint's Safe Lock Company of Cincinnati, Robbins and Appleton Watch Case Company, and the Springfield Illinois Watch Company. Sylvanus Sawyer retired in 1889 to concentrate on his greenhouse and gardens. By this time Gilmer Crowell had moved to New York to make watch cases.

Sylvanus's nephew, Burnside Ellsworth Sawyer, named after the two generals who came from the Department of the Army to view the rifled cannon before the Civil War, took over and inherited the company when Sylvanus died. Burnside had been an engineer and tool designer for L.S. Starrett in Athol, Massachusetts and had started his own company, the Sawyer Tool Company. He merged the watch tool company with his own and moved them to larger quarters on Winter Street. An 1892 catalog shows the Sawyer Tool Manufacturing Company's line of over a hundred different machinist measuring devices, such as rulers, guages, and caliphers.

In 1901, Burnside sold the company to Carl Hubbell who had been superintendent of Simonds Saw. Under Hubbell's ownership, in an effort to settle labor disputes within the company, a policy known as "Sawyerism" was instituted, that allowed for machinists to earn shares in ownership of the company and have a say in how the company was run. Hubbell moved the operation to his hometown of Ashburnham, Massachusetts in 1912, where they continued to make measuring tools until they merged with the T.R. Almond Company, also one of Hubbell's companies, which had previously moved from Brooklyn, New York.

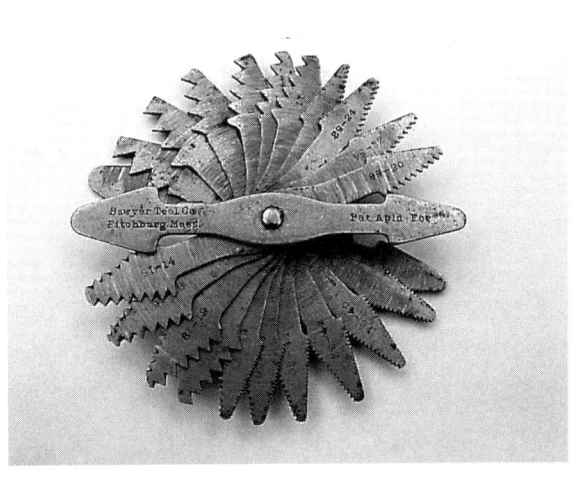

Screw pitch gauge made and sold by the Sawyer Tool Manufacturing Company in the 1890s.

The Fitchburg Watch

Chapter 8

THE WATCH

By the 1870s there were many different grades of watches being manufactured and sold. American watches, mass-produced in the nineteenth century, can be roughly sorted into four categories with respect to the quality or grade of the product. Each of these very general categories is characterized mainly by the market to which it is aimed, and to some extent by the number of pieces manufactured and sold. A look at the attributes of the watches in each of these four categories will provide a general window into the state of the art in the 1870s, and will also show where the Fitchburg Watch fits into it.

Sorting the watches in this way does not define one company over another. All major companies manufactured, or planned to manufacture, lines of different grades. Companies like Waltham, Elgin, and Rockford, for example, whose most popular lines were medium grade, also produced high-quality lines that competed with E. Howard & Co., who only made higher-quality watches. And companies like Waterbury and New York Standard, whose biggest lines were inexpensive grades, also made and sold medium grade watches that could compete with Waltham and Elgin in the latter part of the century.

The first category, later to become the largest category, is what, after the 1870s, came to be called the *dollar watch.* This category includes watches containing no jewels or at most one jewel and, along with the dollar watch, were made as cheaply as possible to supply an increasing demand from a growing populace. A watch in this category, for the most part, was made with a flat balance spring, conical pivots, pin pallet lever or duplex escapement, minimal decoration or finish on the top plate, and often came with a paper dial. For accuracy, it would need to be cleaned and oiled at least every six months, and then it could only be expected to run from two to four years with continual usage before the unjeweled pivots showed wear. Even a relatively new, cleaned, and oiled watch in this category would lose about a minute a day. Begun in the latter part of the century with companies like Waterbury and Ingersoll, these watches ultimately outsold all other watches at a two to one ratio by the 1930s.

The second category might be called the "everyman's watch." These are the bread-and-butter lines of all the major successful manufacturers such as Waltham, Elgin, Illinois, Hampden, Columbus, and Hamilton. The Waltham *soldier's watch* would fit into this category, as would some of the earlier *railroad watches* of companies like Illinois and Rockford. This watch was made with a minimum of 7 jewels, but occasionally contained up to 15 jewels. It came with a flat balance spring, cylindrical pivots, jeweled-pallet escapement, some decoration on the top plate, and an enamel or, in the twentieth century, a metal dial. It needed cleaning and oiling at least once a year, and the 7 jewel version would also last roughly two to four years before the brass pivots began to wear to an oblong shape. It generally lost or gained about thirty seconds a day. By 1900, these watches had far outdistanced the other categories in number of pieces sold, but were later outdistanced by the lesser expensive category.

Category three would be the better grade of watch made by each of the major companies and by some that dedicated their efforts only to these types of timepieces. With these lines, more care, including more handwork, was given to construction, as well as a better grade of materials used. As stated earlier, in the 1870s, E. Howard & Co. only made watches in this category. Railroad watches made by companies like Illinois, Rockford, and Waltham would qualify here, also. This grade came with at least 15 jewels, cylindrical pivots, and a nicely finished balance spring, some of which, by the late 1870s, were constructed with an overcoil. A watch in this grade normally had handsomely finished lever escapements, and high-quality enamel dials. It lost or gained no more than 5 to 10 seconds a day if cleaned and oiled every two years. And an individual watch could be expected to last forever. These timepieces were aimed at either a specialty market, like the railroad men who insisted on a high degree of accuracy, or else a more well-to-do clientele. The number of pieces manufactured and sold was significantly less than the other two categories, while the price per piece was significantly higher.

The last category is reserved for those few watches mass-produced in the latter part of the 1800s to which such care was given, in both design and construction, that they stood out far above all others. Relatively few very-high-quality watches were mass-produced, often being presentation pieces, or made as marketing pieces to show off the level of a company's proven or potential expertise. Often, the first few watches made by a company attained this status. Warren Manufacturing Co.'s 8-day "Howard, Davis and Dennison," the company's presentation watch, was supposed to be in the grouping but, unfortunately, was not. Elgin produced a few "B. W. Raymonds" in this category when they got going in the 1860s.

The highest priced watch in the country by the 1870s was the United States Watch Company of Marion grade of 19-jewel watch called simply the "United States Watch Co." which they introduced in 1869. Whether or not the design and construction of this line of watches warranted such a price can be argued, but there is no question it was a cut above all other grades being manufactured. The most popular watch in this top category was the Waltham 21-jewel Model 72. The first few Illinois 15- and 17-jewel "Stuarts" and "Bunns" might go here, also. And Elgin came out with their 21-jewel Interchangeable in 1876, which some experts have argued was one of the finest mechanical watches mass-produced in America.

This last category must also include the Fitchburg Watch, which, though there is *only one in the line*, ranks with the finest American watches of the nineteenth century. The exterior appearance of the case and dial, while being nicely appointed, is fairly plain in appearance. But a look at the inner workings of the mechanism will show that this watch reflects the peak of American craftsmanship. This is a "watchmaker's watch." It was meant to be taken apart and shown—or shown off—to experts knowledgeable enough to be able to appreciate the design, the materials, and the effort that went into making it. In the manufacture of this watch, Fitchburg was following in the tradition of major watch manufacturers whose best watch was often their first watch. It served the purpose of attracting investors as well as making an impression on a buying public.

The Fitchburg Watch was made by a master. Henry J. Lowe had thirty years experience behind him as a watchmaker, the last six years overseeing the manufacture of all of the United States/Marion company's watches, including their masterpieces. The United States Watch Company grade 18-size, 19-jewel, ¾ plate came out coincident with Lowe's assumption of the superintendency in 1869. And it was during his tenure that the machinery was constructed for the making of the 16-size, ¼ plate and bridge movement. The manufacture of the Fitchburg Watch replicated Marion's highest grade of 16-size, 15-jewel, to which Lowe added a few, even higher grade, touches that increased not only the functionality of the piece but also its beauty.

When Fred Selchow made his comparison between the Fitchburg Watch and the United States Watch Company's "Edwin Rollo" back in 1968, he determined that the two must have been made by the same machinery. He based this on the identical screw pattern holding the top plate, plus the identical design of the pillar plate. He was correct; they were in fact made by the same machinery. And, since the top plate is engraved with the words "Fitchburg, Mass" and the machinery for the 16-size movement was acquired by Sylvanus Sawyer and brought to Fitchburg, Selchow, and other experts after him, assumed—and rightly so—that this watch was manufactured in Fitchburg.

There lingered some doubt, though, that the movement could have been manufactured on that machinery before it left Marion, New Jersey and then assembled, adjusted and engraved in Fitchburg. The parts could have left the bankrupt Marion plant along with the machinery. However, a closer examination of the Fitchburg movement reveals some very interesting details, leading to the conclusion that, though the larger pieces of the Fitchburg Watch were manufactured from the same machinery as those of the Marion watches, it is highly unlikely that they were made in the Marion plant. The details further point up the fact that, with the extraordinary care put into the production of the Fitchburg Watch, it could only have been made by a master craftsman whose intention must have been to have it ranked with the finest watches in this country.

Some similarities beyond the top plate and the pillar plate can be found between the "Edwin Rollo," the "United States Watch Company" and the Fitchburg. First, all three are what was categorized as a 16-size watch but were actually 17-size. Production categories in those days were of even sizes, for example, 14-size, 16-size, 18-size, but these categories often included the odd size just above it. The movements of all three watches are in fact 1 and 22/30 of an inch in diameter, which is 17-size.

All three watches are 15 jewels, which was still considered a fully jeweled watch in the 1870s. By all standards, it was understood among expert watchmakers that anything above 15 jewels was not necessary for accurate and durable functioning. Watches with 15 jewels were not marked as such, but were engraved with the words *Fully Jeweled* until the time when manufacturers began increasing the number of jewels for the purpose of increasing potential market desirability. As late as the 1880s, Edward Howard himself was noted as stating that, as long as he was in charge of the E. Howard & Company, no watch would ever have more than 15 jewels. Clearly, he saw that the demand for his watches would continue to be based on the quality of their construction and not on marketing hype.

Besides the top plates and the pillar plates on the Fitchburg and the Marion watches, it is very likely that the balance cocks were also turned out on the same equipment. The three cocks each have three mounting posts in the exact location on the bottom of the foot. Once made though, the Fitchburg cock is used in a different fashion than the two Marion cocks. The Marion watches have off-cock regulators and the cocks themselves are stepped from the foot to the table. The Fitchburg has an on-cock regulator with an index and scale requiring that the cock not be stepped.

Other similarities can be found between the Marion and Fitchburg watches in three of the wheels. The 3rd, 2nd, and escape wheels of each watch are exactly the same diameter and look to be identical. Also, the dials were very likely made by the same dial company, which would not be at all unusual, even though the design of the numbers on the face are slightly different.

A major overall difference between the Fitchburg and the Marion watches is in the serial numbering. The "United States Watch Co." grade and the Edwin Rollo grade, the only Marion watches that have shown up in the

16 size, have serial numbers on the top plate. Numbers stamped on the pillar plate, the pallet bridge, the minute wheel, the balance arms, the balance cock, and the main spring barrel all correspond to the top plate number. The Fitchburg has no numbers on any piece within the entire movement of the watch. In other words, there are no serial numbers anywhere.

This absence of numbers is, in itself, a rare phenomenon in the manufacture of watches. By the end of the eighteenth century, all watches, whether American or European, whether mass produced in large quantities, or *hand made* in small quantities, have serial numbers either stamped or engraved on them. Even watches that were made as first-run production pieces were given serial numbers. The Nashua Watch Company's first watch, for example, was engraved with the number 1001, even though, reportedly, no watches were actually placed on the market. Rockford's first watch has "No. 1" on it. Adams & Perry engraved No. 1 on its first watch even though the movement was never completed. Elgin National's first watch has the number 101. The Warren Manufacturing Co., which became the Waltham Watch Company, numbered its first watches 1 through 17. Pitkin and Goddard both numbered theirs, probably beginning with the number 1, since pieces with numbers as low as the single digits have been found. After the eighteenth century, all European watchmakers numbered their watches. At least, it is possible to say that no antique watch made after 1800 has ever shown up at an auction, or in anyone's collection, that does not have a serial number of some kind, if not on the top plate, at least somewhere in the movement.

When the Independent Watch Company bought machinery and stock from the bankrupt United States/ Marion Watch Company, they sold watches with top plate serial numbers in a sequence continued from the New Jersey company. It was not until they began making their own top plates, as the Fredonia Watch Co., that they initiated their own numbering sequence. This continuance of serial numbers was not an unusual thing to do. When the New York Watch Company became Springfield, and then later became Hampden, serial numbers continued in sequence from one company to the next. The same can be seen in the transition from the Newark Watch Company to the Cornell Watch Company to the California Watch Company.

It is most likely that serial numbers were added to top plates and pillar plates as they were being made. Stamping a number on the underside of a plate needed to be done early in its existence since the stamping itself raised a ridge of metal around the number which then needed to be "finished" along with the rest of the plate. When machinery was moved to a new company, an inventory of already-stamped plates made on that machine quite often went with it.

The Fitchburg company chose not to use whatever top plates Marion had on hand, but to make their own. The inventory of top plates, still held by the defunct Marion company, were used by the Empire City Watch Company, which attempted to sell nine different grades of 16 size, 1/ 4 plate and bridge watches, ranging in retail selling price from $33.50 up to $450.00 for a movement only. These top plates follow Marion's number sequence, have the same five-screw pattern as the Fitchburg, and had to have been made before the machinery went to Fitchburg, with the movements then being assembled at the Empire City's address at Maiden Lane in New York City.

The dial on the Fitchburg watch is very similar to the Edwin Rollo, but numerals on the Fitchburg are shorter and there are decorations on the seconds hand dial of the Fitchburg. One significant difference in the dial between the Fitchburg and the Marion watches is in how they are attached to the pillar plate. The Fitchburg has three dial attachment screws. The Edwin Rollo has two pinned posts and a Swiss-style dog screw from the side. The United States Watch Company model has dog screws that go down from the top plate. The older, more traditional method of attaching the dial to the pillar plate is the use of pinned posts, two to four posts that fit into holes in the plate and are then held in place by tapered brass pins. Just coming into use at that time, the Fitchburg's style of attachment are screws that come in from the side of the pillar plate and hold the posts in place. Elgin had already began using them in the early 1870s. The Waltham Model 72 has screws on the side, but their Crescent Street Model 1870 has posts and pins. Later, by the 1880s, the style of attachment as seen on the Fitchburg Watch had become commonplace.

Other comparisons show the difference in construction between the watches made in the Marion plant and the one made in Fitchburg. The mainspring barrel on the Fitchburg is larger in circumference, and the Marion watches have "patent applied for" engraved on the barrel cover. This patent would be for Marion's reversible barrel. On the Fitchburg, the great wheel is at the very top of the barrel, and on the Marion watches it is a third of the way down from the top. The highly polished and beveled recess well and hub boss on the Fitchburg minute wheel is smaller than on the Marion watches. Also, the ratchet wheel on the Fitchburg is a different circumference, plus being beveled and highly polished. The arbor for the 2nd wheel is shorter on the Fitchburg. The 3rd wheel has a more delicate pinion, and the 4th wheel has a shorter pinion, even though the circumference of these wheels are the same from one watch to the other.

Like the "United States Watch Co." grade, the Fitchburg top plate, pillar plate and balance cock are all nickel plated. The top side of the top plate is very nicely machine damaskeened, as are both sides of the pillar plate. Even the recessed wells for the minute and hour wheels on the under side of the pillar plate are damaskeened, as are the wells on the top side of the pillar plate.

The construction and the materials used in the movements of both the "United States Watch Co." grade of the Marion and the Fitchburg Watch show that they were both meant to be of the highest quality. The top edge of the roller table in each is beveled and the roller table itself is highly polished, as is the minute wheel pinion. The pivot jewel setting for the 3rd wheel is solid gold, as are the settings for the escape wheel and the 4th wheel. The edges of the ratchet wheel, the minute wheel hub boss and the recess well, plus the escape wheel shaft, are all beveled. This kind of finishing on the stem wind version of Marion's "United States Watch Co." grade of 16-size 19-jewel ¼ plate and bridge movement could justify a retail price of $480 in 1872.

The Marion watches use Elson's double index regulator, while the Fitchburg has a standard single index on-cock regulator, beveled and highly polished. Even though some of the more complicated and more exact micrometer regulators had come into use before this time, they always involved a manufacturer having to pay fees to whomever invented them. George P. Reed obtained the patent in 1865 for the first micrometer regulator, using a whiplash spring, even though it is universally accepted that Charles Fasoldt's invention of his micrometer regulator preceded Reed's by a year. Fasoldt's regulator, though, like John Fitch's steamboat patents, was deemed impractical and not used by any other watchmaker. Reed, on the other hand, who worked for E. Howard & Co., received a fee, either from Howard or any other company, every time his patented whiplash spring regulator was used. Frederick Giles also held a patent for the micrometer regulator used on products from the United States Watch Company. This regulator was a somewhat complicated affair, a little too complicated maybe, because very few other manufacturers used either this or a similar design.

Henry J. Lowe obviously opted not to use a regulator for which the company would have to pay a patent fee. But they were certainly in good company using a standard regulator on a high-quality watch. It was uncommon to find anything but a standard regulator on any Continental watch in the 1870s, and very rare to find a ¾-plate English watch with a micrometer regulator. Even the best products made in Europe, such as those made by Frodsham in England and Swiss companies like Patek Phillipe, or Ekegren had simple index regulators, with few exceptions. In America, most railroad watches, up until the 1890s, still carried simple index regulators. Regulating a movement to the degree of accuracy that would necessitate a micrometer adjustment was, like the use of more than 15 jewels, more of a marketing ploy than a necessity for a watch that lost or gained no more than a few seconds a day.

Balance cock and regulator

Several features of the Fitchburg Watch balance mechanism would be found only on a watch of the highest grade. The decorative engraving on the balance cock is very delicate, and compares to the engraving on "United States Watch Co." grade. The cap jewel setting on the Fitchburg and the pivot jewel settings on its balance are made of gold, as are all the temperature and timing screws on the balance wheel. The balance staff and the arms of the pallet are highly polished. The entry and exit jewels are nicely rounded.

The balance lever is exquisite. The pallet arms are narrowly and finely cut, and very possibly the most delicate arms to be found on any American-made watch. The pallet itself is highly polished with beveled edges. The counterpoise on the lever is composed of graceful and delicate arms that are beveled and honed to extremely fine points.

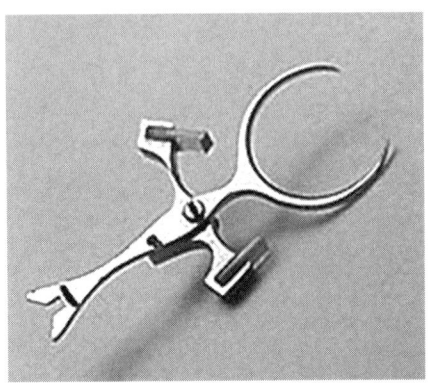

*Pallet on the Fitchburg Watch,
showing the delicate pallet arms and
the counterpoise.*

One innovation on the Fitchburg Watch can be found on only a few of the highest grade American watches made up until that time. This is what was known as a "floating balance spring stud," so called because it was free to move prior to its attachment to the balance cock which is installed after the balance assembly is placed in the movement. This method of attaching the balance spring appears to be an extra little touch, used in America on only a few of the highest grade watches. Most all American mass-produced ¾-plate watches made before the 1890s had the balance spring attached to the cock with a post held in place by a screw coming in from the side. This made for easier manufacture but increased the risk of the delicate balance spring being damaged during servicing. Higher-grade Swiss watches, such as those made by Patek Phillipe, used a similar floating stud arrangement, and by the twentieth century it became a standard in all American watches.

188

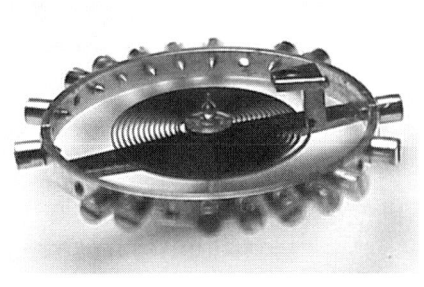

Balance spring (hair spring) stud

The utilization of this type of spring stud, as well as the delicate pallet arms and many other features of the watch, show that Lowe was obviously attempting to make what would be considered as one of the finest watches of its day. When the "Mr. Lawrence" from New York gave his opinion of the plans for Lowe's watch to the Fitchburg Board of Trade in the spring of 1875, saying that they were as fine as anything he'd seen in Europe, his testimony was not wrong in the least. The watch that Henry J. Lowe built from those plans was equal to anything produced on either side of the ocean up to that time.

Although working in relative obscurity in his one-man watchmaker's shop in Fitchburg for twenty-two years before going to work for the United States Watch Company, it appears that Henry J. Lowe's one interest in life, other than his family, lay in the movement of the pocket watch. The uprooting of his family and leaving the security of his hometown to go work for Frederick Giles in New Jersey must have been inspired by his and Giles' mutual interest in producing the country's finest watch. The opportunity offered him by Sylvanus Sawyer and the Fitchburg Board of Trade, the potential of building the country's finest watch right there in his own home town, must have seemed to him like an arrangement made in heaven.

Since the plans for Lowe's watch were based on Marion's best grade of 16-size movement, developed under his supervision as the highest priced watch in the country, he must be given credit for the design and construction of the Fitchburg Watch.

In some ways the Fitchburg Watch reflects the character of Henry J. Lowe. A quiet, unassuming family man, he helped to further the perception of his craft as an art form. And the Fitchburg Watch, while serviceable but plain on the outside, should be characterized on the inside as a work of art.

The wear on the watch's original hunter case shows that it was probably used for years by Henry's son, Frank, and possibly Frank's son. For at least the last forty years, it has been quiet, kept in storage, but after recently being cleaned and oiled, it took off running with the same sprightliness as it must have done a century ago.

Bibliography

Abbot. Henry G. *Watch Factories of America*, Chicago, 1883.

Anderson, Larry, *Directions of a Town, A History of Harvard, Massachusetts*, Harvard Common Press, 1976.

Blewett, Mary H., *Constant Turmoil, The Politics of Industrial Life in 19th Century New England*, University of Massachusetts Press, 2001.

Bolina, August C. *The Watchmakers of Massachusetts*, Washington, D.C., Kensington Historical Press, 1987.

Cochran, Thomas C., *Frontiers of Change, Early Industrialization in America*, New York, 1981.

Cochran, Thomas C., and William Miller, *The Age of Enterprise, A Social History of Industrial America*, New York, 1942.

Crossman, Charles S., *The Complete History of Watchmaking in America*, Jewellers Circular and Horological Review, 1885-87.

Currier, Frederick, *History of the Board of Trade*, manuscript, Fitchburg Historical Society.

Daniels, George, and Cecil Clutton, *Watches*, New York, Viking Press, 1965.

Davis, Lance E. et al., *American Economic Growth, An Economist's History of the United States*, New York, Harper and Row, 1972.

Dawley, Alan, *Class and Community: The Industrial Revolution in Lynn*, Cambridge, Massachusetts,1976.

Douglass, Elisha P., *The Coming of Age of American Business, Three Centuries of Enterprise, 1600-1900*, Chapel Hill, 971.

Dunbar, Seymour, *A History of Travel in America*, Indianapolis, Bobbs-Merrill, 1915.

Emerson, William, *Fireside Legends*, Fitchburg Historical Society, 1900.

Emerson, William, *Fitchburg Past and Present*, Fitchburg Historical Society, 1903.

Faler, Paul G. *Mechanics and Manufacturers in the Early Industrial Revolution: Lynn, Massachusetts, 1780-1860*, Albany, 1981.

Faulkner, Harold U., *American Economic History*, New New Harper and Brothers, 1949.

Fitchburg Board of Trade, *The Project of Organizing a Company for the Manufacture of Watches in this City*, Committee Report, 2nd Annual Report, 1876.

Fosdick, Charles, *The Sawyer Gun*, manuscript, Fitchburg Historical Society.

Gies, Joseph and Frances, *The Ingenious Yankees*, New York, 1976.

Gutman, Herbert G., *Work, Culture, and Society in Industrializing America, Essays in American Working-class Social History 1815-1920*, New York, Knopf, 1975.

Habakkuk, H. J., *American and British Technology in the Nineteenth Century: The Search for Labour-saving Inventions*, Cambridge, UK, 1962.

Harrold, Michael C., *American Watchmaking, A Technical History of the American Watch Industry, 1850-1930*, Columbia, Pennsylvania, NAMCC Bulletin, 1984.

Hawke, David Freeman, *Nuts and Bolts of the Past, A History of American Technology, 1776-1860*, New York, Harper and Row, 1988.

Hindle, Brooke, *Emulation and Invention*, New York, New University Press, 1981.

Hindle, Brooke and Steven Lubar, *Engines of Change, The American Industrial Revolution, 1790-1860*, Washington, D.C.,Smithsonian Press, 1986.

Hirsch, Susan E., *Roots of the American Working Class: Industrialization of Crafts in Newark, 1800-1860*, Philadelphia, University of Pennsylvania Press, 1978.

Hounshell, David A. *From the American System to Mass-production, 1800-1932*, Baltimore, Johns Hopkins University Press, 1984.

Hurd, D. Hamilton, ed., *History of Worcester County, Massachusetts, with Biographical Sketches of many of its Pioneers and Prominent Men,* Philadelphia, J.W. Lewis & Co., 1889.

Hunter, Louis C., *A History of Industrial Power in the United States, 1780-1930*, Vol.I and Vol.II, Greenville, Delaware, 1979.

Jay, Peter, *The Wealth of Man*, New York, Public Affairs, 2000.

Jeremy, David, *Artisans, Entrepreneurs, and Machines*, London, Ashgate Publishing Ltd., 1998.

Kasson, John F., *Civilizing the Machine: Technology and Republican Values in America, 1776-1900*, New York, 1976.

Kirkpatrick, Doris, *The City and the River*, Fitchburg Historical Society, 1971.

Landes, David S., *Revolution in Time, Clocks and the Making of the Modern World*, Cambridge, Massachusetts, Harvard University Press, 1983.

Larkin, Jack, *The Reshaping of Everyday Life, 1790-1840*, New York, Harper and Row, 1988.

Lee, Susan Previant, and Peter Passell, *A New Economic View of American History*, New York, W.W. Norton & Co., 1979.

Massachusetts Dental Association, *The Story of Dentistry in Massachusetts, 1864 to 1964.*

Milham, Willis I., *Time and Timekeepers*, New York, MacMillan, 1944.

Montgomery, David, *Beyond Equality: Labor and the Radical Republicans, 1862-1872*, Urbana, University of Illinois Press, 1981.

Moore, Charles W. *Timing of a Century, History of the Waltham Watch Company*, Cambridge, Massachusetts, Harvard University Press, 1945.

Muir, William, and Bernard Kraus, *Marion, A History of the United States Watch Company*, Columbia, Pennsylvania, NAWCC, 1980.

Nevins, Allen, *The Emergence of Modern America, 1865-1878* New York, MacMillan, 1927.

Nijssen, Gerrit A., *F.A. Lange and Glashutte*, Boston, 1978.

North, Douglas C., *Economic Growth of the United States, 1790-1860*, New York, 1961.

O'Malley, Michael, *Keeping Watch, A History of American Time*, New York, Penguin Books, 1990.

Output, Employment, and Productivity in the United States after 1800, *Studies in Income and Wealth, Volume 30*, New York, Columbia University Press, 1966.

Prager, Frank D., *The Autobiography of John Fitch*, Philadelphia, The American Philosophical Society, 1976.

Roe, James Wickham, *English and American Tool Builders*, New York, 1926.

Rosenberg, Nathan, *Technology and American Economic Growth*, New York, 1972.

Salisbury, Stephen, *The State, the Investor, and the Railroad: the Boston & Albany, 1825-1867,* Cambridge, Massachusetts, Harvard University Press, 1967.

Skousen, Mark, and M.E. Sharpe, *The Making of Modern Economics*, New York, 2001.

Smith, Cyril S., *From Art to Science: Seventy-two Objects Illustrating the Nature of Discovery,* Cambridge, MA, 1980.

Sobel, Robert, *Panic on Wall Street*, London, 1961.

Taylor, George Rogers, *The Transportation Revolution, 1815-1860*, New York, Holt, Rinehart, 1951.

Taussig, Frank W., *The Tariff History of the United States*, New York, G.P. Putnam & Sons, 1931.

Temin, Peter, *General Factors in American Economic Growth in the Nineteenth Century*, New York, 1975.

Willis, Henry A., *The Early Days of the Railroads in Fitchburg*, Fitchburg, Sentinel Printing Co., 1894.

Woodbury, Robert S., *Studies in the History of Machine Tools*, Cambridge, Massachusetts, 1972.

Index

199

201

202

203